With Custer in '74

James Calhoun's Diary of the Black Hills Expedition

Edited by Lawrence A. Frost

Brigham Young University Press

Library of Congres Cataloging in Publication Data

Calhoun, James, 1845–1876.
With Custer in '74.

Includes bibliographical references and index.
1. Black Hills, S. D. & Wyo.—Description and travel.
2. Calhoun, James, 1845–1876. 3. Custer, George
Armstrong, 1839–1876. 4. United States. Army.
7th Cavalry—Biography. 5. Indians of North America—
Wars—1866–1896—Personal narratives. I. Frost,
Lawrence A. II. Title.
F657.B6C343   978.3'9   79-13132
ISBN 0-8425-1620-4

International Standard Book Number: 0-8425-1620-4
Brigham Young University Press, Provo, Utah 84602

79   1.5Mc   32698

To
Hugh Shick
the Inspirator

Contents

Acknowledgments

The late R. G. Cartwright, noted Custer battle and Black Hills historian of St. Petersburg, Florida, shared with me his extensive knowledge of the Black Hills expedition.

John M. Carroll of Bryan, Texas, was always willing to advise me and to tactfully suggest possible avenues to follow.

Mrs. Jack Jennette, my secretary, took upon herself the tedious task of typing the manuscript, and in her alertness caught many errors.

Colonel George S. Pappas, former director of the United States Army Military History Research Collection at Carlisle Barracks, was, as always, very helpful.

I am particularly indebted to the staffs of the Monroe County Library System, the Dorsch Memorial Library of Monroe, the Michigan State Library, and the University of Michigan Library.

And I am very grateful to the following for their assistance: Archibald Hanna, curator, Bienecke Rare Book and Manuscript Library, Yale University Library; John Mullane, Cincinnati Public Library; Gene Gressley, director, and David Crosson, research librarian, Western History Research Center, University of Wyoming; J. D. Young, former historian, Custer Battlefield Na-

tional Monument; Marie T. Capps, United States Military
Academy Library; Don Russell, editor, Chicago Westerner's
Brand Book; Bart R. Voigt, director, Wyoming State Historical
Department; Nyle H. Miller, former director, Kansas State His-
torical Society; Sam Gilluly, director, Montana Historical So-
ciety; Oliver H. Ohr, manuscript division, Library of Congress;
Elaine C. Everly, Old Army Branch, National Archives; Gary L.
Morgan, Cartographic Archives, National Archives; Charlotte A.
Palmer, Audiovisual Archives, National Archives; B. William
Henry, Fort Larned National Historic Site; Dr. John Y. Simon,
director, the Ulysses S. Grant Association; Leigh G. DeLay, his-
torian, Nebraska State Historical Society; Archie Motley, Chi-
cago Historical Research Center; Frank E. Vyzralek, archivist,
State Historical Society of North Dakota; Mr. and Mrs. Clay
Curran, Lead, South Dakota; Cameron E. Ferweda, Custer,
South Dakota; Mrs. Helen Hershaw, Toledo Public Library;
Mrs. Richard White and Mrs. Barbara Tierney, Monroe County
Library System; Dayton W. Canaday, director, and Mrs. Bonnie
Gardner, photo curator, South Dakota Historical Research Cen-
ter; John Drayton, managing editor, Brigham Young University
Press; Frank J. Shideler, agricultural editor, South Dakota State
University; Roy Hamlin, *Monroe Evening News*; Dr. Donald R.
Progulske, University of Massachusetts.

A special expression of gratitude is due Kathryn Frandsen
and Howard A. Christy, of the editorial staff of Brigham Young
University Press, for their patience, perception and skill.

Lawrence A. Frost

Introduction

The Black Hills are a magnificent mass of mountains, elliptical in shape and 4,500 square miles in size, forming the easternmost ridge of the Rocky Mountains in southwestern South Dakota. This geologist's paradise is among the earth's oldest features in North America. Literally an island in the vast Great Plains, the hills were known to the Sioux, Cheyenne and Arapahoe Indians as Paha Sapa, Sioux words meaning hills of black. The large tracts of yellow pine (ponderosa) that cover outer surfaces of the Hills give the impression, when viewed from the Plains, of being black.

An enigma to everyone, the Hills stood tantalizing and unexplored. From time to time stories of gold discoveries within them had passed among the settlers and Eastern military posts. There were unexplainable secrets locked in that strange and forbidding area that lured the adventurous and seduced the avaricious. It had been rumored along the frontier that only a few white men had penetrated its outer rim and none had lived to tell of it.[1]

---

1. Lawrence A. Frost, *The Custer Album* (Seattle: Superior Publ. Co., 1964), p. 128.

The Treaty of 1868 had set aside nearly 43,000 square miles as a Sioux reservation. The most valuable portion was the Black Hills which bound its western border. The Sioux regarded them as a religious sanctuary or asylum and believed it would be bad medicine for anyone who entered.

The Hills offered no temptation to the Indians. Women ventured inside to cut tepee poles, and some hunting was undertaken on the fringes, but no one regarded it as home. The frequent rains and the formidable thunder and lightning storms were not conducive to camping comfort. Also, horses were easily lost in the nearly impenetrable thickets choking much of the rough and broken terrain.

Colonel Richard I. Dodge observed in 1875 that Indians never had lived in the Black Hills, would not live in them, and did not care for them. They informed Dodge that the hills would have been given to the whites but for the urging of "squaw men" who insisted, when the Government made an approach to buy them, that a big fuss on the part of the Indians would get them a big price.[2]

In 1858 Lieutenant G. K. Warren, who was to achieve fame at the Battle of Gettysburg, completed his report of the 1855, 1856 and 1857 explorations of Nebraska and Dakota. In it he drew attention to the necessity of advancing American settlements and displacing Indians in the interest of national development. Warren prophetically concluded:

> There are so many inevitable causes at work to produce a war with the Dakotas before many years, that I regard the greatest fruits of the explorations I have conducted to be the knowledge of the proper routes by which to invade their country and conquer them. The Black Hills is the great point in their territory at which to strike all the Teton Dakotas, except the Brules and Okandandas. Here they can assemble their largest force, and here I believe they would make a stand. In the event of another outbreak, a post should be established at the Mouth of the Shyenne, on the north side, from which to operate simultaneously with troops from Fort Laramie.... They will not, I think, permit the occupation of the vicinity of these hills without offering a determined resistance."[3]

2. Richard I. Dodge, *The Black Hills* (New York: J. Miller, 1876), p. 138.

3. Lieutenant G. K. Warren, *Preliminary Report of Explorations in Nebraska and Dakota in the Years 1855-56-57* (Washington, D.C.: Government Printing Office, 1875).

During the fifties gold and silver strikes were made all over the West, from Canada to Arizona, and with them came the population incursions such announcements bring. Near the end of the Civil War gold was discovered in Montana, then in Idaho, and the inevitable rushes immediately followed. After the war a veritable horde of prospectors invaded the West. Tent cities mushroomed wherever there was a prospect or a dream of easy wealth, some in the most unusual places. One contemporary citizen observed: "Congregate a hundred Americans anywhere beyond the settlements and they immediately lay out a city and apply for admission to the Union, while 25 of them become candidates for the United States Senate."[4]

The Sioux effectively demonstrated their resentment to the white inroads in 1862 by a bloody raid on the settlers in southern Minnesota. Following the slaughter they withdrew to northwestern Dakota, then proceeded to the east side of the Big Horn Mountains where they seized most of the Crow lands.

Not to be outdone by the bloodbath in Minnesota, Colonel J. M. Chivington and the First Colorado Cavalry on November 29, 1864, attacked an encampment of about 500 peaceful men, women and children, slaughtering large numbers of them. Chivington's brutal attack provoked vicious retaliation throughout the frontier east of the Rockies.[5]

These raids reached a peak when the Sioux led by Crazy Horse audaciously attacked a wood train escort of 81 officers and men of Col. H. B. Carrington's command at Fort Phil Kearney on December 21, 1866. There were no survivors of the detail led by Capt. William J. Fetterman.[6]

Following the defeat of Carrington's forces at Fort Kearney Chief Red Cloud's warriors maintained a formidable siege along the central part of the Bozeman Trail. In August 1867 Red Cloud suffered severe losses in an attempt to annihilate a woodcutting party of 32 soldiers and civilians six miles from Fort Kearney. Using 14 wagon boxes as breastworks, the woodcutters

4. Albert D. Richardson, *Beyond the Mississippi...* (Hartford: American Publ. Co., 1867), p. 77.

5. Thomas D. Clark, *Frontier America; the Story of the Westward Movement* (New York: Charles Scribner's Sons, 1959), p. 701; and O. O. Howard, *My Life and Experiences among Our Hostile Indians*, Hartford: n.p., 1907) p. 488.

6. U.S. Congress, Senate, *Executive Document 33*, 50th Cong., 1st sess., pp. 39–41.

stood off nearly 2,500 warriors, killing or wounding about 300. An officer and two privates were killed and another man was wounded. Still, Red Cloud continued his siege as long as the forts along the Bozeman Trail existed.

In 1868 a treaty was drawn at Fort Laramie apparently admitting defeat. The Government agreed to abandon Forts Reno, Smith and Kearney along the Bozeman Trail. In addition to a pledge of peace, the Sioux agreed to relinquish the land north of the Platte River if hunting rights were assured. They also agreed not to hinder railroad construction. General Sherman observed some months later that the peace conference had been "an error of judgment." He believed the Indians should have been punished by confiscating stolen goods in their possession and putting all the Sioux under the rigid control of civil agents.[7]

Hardly had the peace commissioners left before both Indian depredations and white encroachments began to undermine all that had been accomplished. It soon became obvious the two races could not live side by side in peace. Councils, treaties and pledges of peace were made frequently (and in good faith) but unscrupulous agents misappropriated food and supplies promised to the Indians, white men disregarded reservation boundaries, and young warriors ignored the treaty terms by continuing their raids on the whites.[8]

There were numerous clashes and engagements between the Indians and the military following the 1868 Laramie Treaty. The frontier settlements, railroad survey and construction crews, and transcontinental travelers were constantly harassed and raided by warriors. By 1874 Crazy Horse, Sitting Bull, and their dissident followers were still out of control. The number of hostile warriors with them fluctuated from 1,500 to 4,000. Chiefs Spotted Tail and Red Cloud, having become two doves in a hostile atmosphere, persuaded many of their chiefs to live a peaceful life at their agencies, but the Sioux depredations continued.[9]

---

7. Mark H. Brown, *The Plainsmen of the Yellowstone* (New York: Putnam, 1961) pp. 184–85.

8. Joseph P. Peters, comp., *Indian Battles and Skirmishes on the American Frontier, 1790–1898* (New York: Argonaut Press, 1966), p. 7.

9. Richard I. Dodge, *Our Wild Indians...* (Hartford: A.D. Worthington & Co., 1883), p. 44.

By 1874 Army intelligence reports warned of serious trouble ahead. It was just a question of where and when. As a result of his explorations in 1855, 1856 and 1857, G. K. Warren had advised that "the Black Hills is the great point in their territory at which to strike all the Teton Dakotas." He warned that war with the Dakotas was inevitable.[10]

By 1874 Sheridan had decided that in order to better control Indians making raids in the Department of the Platte it would be necessary "to establish a large military post in the country known as the Black Hills, so that by holding an interior point in the heart of the Indian country the troops could threaten the villages and stock of the Indians if the latter raided the settlements."[11]

On April 24, General Sheridan, accompanied by General Alfred Terry, visited Custer at Fort Lincoln to discuss the proposed expedition. Terry, probably because of his legal training, at first thought it inappropriate to consider a reconnaissance of the Black Hills until it was decided that the Government was within its rights to enter that part of the Sioux reservation. After considerable study he threw in his support.

The biggest problem was funding. Custer jumped to the rescue by submitting that there was a way to conduct the reconnaissance without additional cost to the Government. He had told Sheridan in the fall of 1873 following the termination of the Yellowstone campaign "that the proposed reconnaissance can be made and result in an actual savings to the Government."[12] Sheridan requested that a letter be addressed to him detailing what Custer had in mind. Such a letter was an absolute necessity in presenting the case to Grant, Sherman, and Secretary of War William W. Belknap. Sheridan knew they were budget conscious at that time. Three days later the necessary information was on its way to Sheridan. Custer had calculated the comparative costs of keeping ten companies in the garrison in contrast to sending them into the field. His figures showed that $19,437 would be saved by foraging along the route the 1,200 horses and mules needed for the expedition. Added ex-

---

10. Warren, *Explorations in Nebraska and Dakota*, p. 53.

11. Philip H. Sheridan, *Record of Engagements with Hostile Indians. . .* (Washington, D.C.: Government Printing Office, 1882), p. 38.

12. George A. Custer to Philip H. Sheridan, April 27, 1874, Calhoun Diary.

penses would be pay for a wagon master, 100 teamsters, and an interpreter, expenses that would still leave a comfortable balance.[13]

Custer also indicated that he had a very reliable Indian guide quite familiar with the Black Hills who knew an entry to the interior that was practicable for wagons. He hoped, he wrote in his conclusion, that he would be notified "as soon as it has become positively determined that this movement is to be made ... [to] have as much time as possible to attend to details."[14]

It is interesting to read in September 8, 1874 edition of the *Chicago Inter-Ocean* that "General Custer had been mistaken only in the amount of the balance, which was found on the return of the expedition to have been over $16,000."

Correspondent William E. Curtis, in reporting for the *New York World* September 12, 1874, wrote that "the Black Hills Expedition had actually saved the Government between $20,000 and $30,000." Relying upon grazing along the route had made the big difference. In the *World's* edition of September 1, he had written, "The Expedition has repaid its cost twenty-fold."

Approval of the expedition was not long in coming. On June 8, 1874, Special Orders No. 117 were issued at St. Paul by Brigadier General Terry directing Lieutenant Col. G. A. Custer to organize an expedition at Fort A. Lincoln, D. T., to reconnoiter a route to Bear Butte (just northeast of the Black Hills) and to explore "the country southeast and southwest of that point."[15] Meanwhile, Custer, with his customary enthusiasm, had become engrossed in his plans for the expedition. He had been requesting equipment, recruits and new arms for some time.

Custer had made every effort to determine the whereabouts and number of potentially hostile Indians. In a communication from Indian Agent John M. Smith[16] he was presented with a comprehensive census of the Sioux and Northern Cheyennes at

13. Ibid.

14. Ibid.

15. William Ludlow, *Report of a Reconnaissance of the Black Hills of Dakota, Made in the Summer of 1874* (Washington, D.C.: Government Printing Office, 1875), p. 8; and U.S. Congress, House, *House Document 2*, 43d Cong. 2d sess., p. 24.

16. John M. Smith to George A. Custer, February 25, 1874, Elizabeth B. Custer Collection, Custer Battlefield National Monument, Crow Agency, Montana.

the different agencies north of the Platte and west of the Missouri rivers. Agent Smith emphatically pointed out that his tally would not correspond with the various agency reports. One can only conclude that the various agents would report many more Indians than were actually at the agencies, a form of padding of reports to secure for them an overage of annuity goods the agents might peddle for their private profit.

Citing a tally of the Spotted Tail, Red Cloud, Lower Brule, Standing Rock and Cheyenne agencies, Smith gave a total of 2,040 lodges housing about 3,060 warriors. He indicated that "fully one-half of the young men have one or more pistols, exclusive of other arms. All have bows and arrows. About one-half of the warriors remaining at the agencies have repeating rifles [Winchester] all others breechloaders. I have known Indians at White River Agency to have as many as 3,000 rounds of ammunition for a single gun . . . . Fully three-fourths of all enumerated are hostile; the bitter ones being old men."[17] From this report Sheridan concluded that the expedition into the Black Hills could meet a belligerent body of as many as 2,500 warriors. This was helpful information for it established the need for a reconnaissance in force.

When it became obvious to the Indians that Custer was preparing an expedition to explore the Black Hills, they were greatly concerned with what they knew would be a violation of their treaty rights. Fifty years later Mrs. Custer recalled how the Sioux chiefs called upon her husband frequently to discuss the situation. "They urged that the white men must not go into the Hills that it was dangerous and would bring on war." The chiefs indicated to General Custer that their people would fight to keep the lands promised to them.[18]

Though Custer respected the chiefs and showed his deference for them by providing a feast on each of these occasions, he profited from their warning by taking with him a large military escort. He firmly believed that the Government should keep its

---

17. Ibid.

18. Elizabeth Bacon Custer, "General Custer and the Indian Chiefs," *The Outlook* (July 27, 1927), p. 408. One Indian, Running Antelope, informed Custer that the Indians objected to the exploration because of their fear that when the mineral and agricultural wealth was determined, the white men would want to take over—evidence that they had an accurate assessment of the white man's character.

promises to the Indians, but he could do no less than obey orders when General Terry ordered him in command of the reconnaissance. A year after the Expedition, while in New York, he said to a reporter of the *New York Herald*: "The success of the reservation system depends on the Government keeping its promises .... The Indians have a strong attachment for the lands containing the bones of their ancestors and dislike to leave it. Love of country is almost a religion with them. It is not the value of the land that they consider, but their strong local attachment that the white man does not feel, and consequently does not respect. He [the Indian] keenly feels the injustice that has been done him, and being of a proud and haughty nature, he resents it."[19]

Eastern newspapers began to run stories on the upcoming expedition, questioning motives and legality, and complaining about the tight security. Terry read all the accounts, then released a statement on July 27 defending the Government's position:

"I am unable to see that any just offense is given to the Indians by the expedition to the Hills. Plunder is not the objective of the expedition; neither is it sent out for the purpose of ascertaining the mineral or agricultural resources of the Black Hills. It seeks neither gold, timber nor arable land."[20]

Terry was offering a pristine conception of what the expedition was intended to accomplish. Though its original objectives were strictly military, expedition staffing indicated considerably more than that.[21] The addition of two practical miners to the expeditionary force is evidence of this altered concept. Custer's reports are glowing evidence of this change of thinking.

When the expeditionary force left Fort Lincoln on July 2, it consisted of ten companies of the Seventh Cavalry; one company of the Twentieth and Seventeenth Infantry; a fire support battery (three Gatling guns and one three-inch cannon); an engineer detachment; a detachment of Indian scouts, guides, inter-

---

19. Dodge, *The Black Hills*, p. 10.

20. George A. Custer to Editor, *Bismarck Tribune*, July 30, 1874; and Herbert Krause and Gary D. Olsen, *Prelude to Glory: A Newspaper Accounting of Custer's 1874 Expedition to the Black Hills* (Sioux Falls, S.D.: Brevet Press, 1974).

21. Ludlow, *Reconnaissance of the Black Hills*, p. 8.

preters and teamsters; and a sixteen-piece band. Supplies were carried in 110 wagons and ambulances. Since it was decided there would be an inadequate supply of game for the hungry troopers, 300 head of cattle were taken along.[22]

Custer's second in command was Major George A. Forsyth of Beecher Island fame. Forsyth commanded five companies of cavalry while Major Joseph Tilford commanded the other five. The two companies of Infantry were commanded by Lieutenant Louis H. Sanger, and the battery of Gatling guns and the Rodman cannon was commanded by Lieutenant Josiah Chance. Lieutenant George D. Wallace was assigned the Indian scouts and Captain William Ludlow commanded the detachment of engineers.

The President's son, Lieutenant Colonel Fred T. Grant, who was serving on General Sheridan's staff at the time, went along for the ride. Both Forsyth and Grant had been asked for by Custer. Why Grant's presence was requested is difficult to determine. He served no useful purpose but spent most of his time in a mild to moderate state of inebriation that harmed no one but himself. Of particular interest was Charlie Reynolds, a well-known scout and hunter, who went along as a guide. It was Reynolds who carried out of the Hills the official report that gold had been discovered.

The expedition was also accompanied by correspondents of five newspapers: the *New York Tribune, Chicago Inter-Ocean, St. Paul Press, St. Paul Pioneer,* and *Bismarck (Dakota Territory) Tribune.* William E. Curtis, of the *Chicago Inter-Ocean,* was particularly instrumental in whipping up interest (after the expedition returned) over the presence of gold in the Black Hills.

Though the expedition's primary purpose was that of obtaining information of military importance, Captain William Ludlow, in charge of the engineer detachment, went to considerable lengths to expand the expedition into a full-fledged exploration, to include staffing to allow in-depth studies of flora and fauna as well as mapping and geology. The services of two well-known geologists were obtained, for example: Newton H. Winchell, state geologist of Minnesota, and George Bird Grinell of Yale University—and their assistants.

22. R. Progylske, *Yellow Ore, Yellow Hair, Yellow Pine* (Brookings, S.D.: South Dakota State University, 1974), pp. 13, 16.

Winchell was not the most compatible geologist for that expedition. Though many expedition members saw or panned gold, Winchell steadfastly maintained he had seen none. Had this been a gold-hunting expedition, Custer surely could have obtained "a more complaisant geologist."[23] One wonders if Custer had heard some rumblings of Winchell's eccentricities and, in an attempt to offset them, had decided to take along the two practical miners, Horatio N. Ross and William McKay. In any event, Winchell contemptuously rejected any statements that gold had been discovered. In this he was supported by Fred Grant who wrote at the end of his final report: "I don't believe that any gold was found at all." It appears that the two miners disregarded Grant's disparaging remarks as to their character and their gold finds, for neither made any remarks to the press as to Grant's continual inebriation and his inability to recognize gold if it had been placed in his hands.

William H. Illingworth of St. Paul was also hired by Ludlow to make a series of stereographic photographs of the Black Hills. In doing so Illingworth provided the basis for a remarkable ecological study made 100 years later.[24]

The expedition accomplished more than was hoped. The topography of southwestern Dakota, southeastern Montana, and northeastern Wyoming was recorded with greater accuracy, the course of all streams was determined, and a comprehensive study of botany, geology and zoology was made of a hitherto

---

23. Watson Parker, "The Majors and the Miners," *Journal of the West* 11(January 1972): 101.

24. Illingworth took over 80 photographs on the Expedition. The original agreement called for six sets of fifty-five stereographic prints. He provided the Government with only one set.

Under the direction of Dr. Donald Progulske, formerly with the South Dakota State University, a study was made to determine the natural and man-made changes in Black Hills vegetation over the past 100 years. By photographing the same scenes in Illingworth's photographs, Progulske was able to compare "then and now."

Striking changes in the ecology were noted the most common being the excessive increase in the forests. The now heavily wooded areas prevent growth of underbrush and ground cover necessary to sustain wild life and restrict water production in streams. From this study it was learned that there can be too many trees in a forest.

Dr. Progulske observed that, "Whoever ordered a photographer to accompany the Black Hills Expedition of 1874—whether it was General Custer himself, Colonel Ludlow, or the Commanding General—unknowingly established a base upon which patterns of the forest can be measured long into the future."

Dr. Progulske heads the Department of Forestry and Wildlife Management at the University of Massachusetts.

unexplored region. Gold and other mineral deposits were veri-
fied and timber, water and soil fertility were studied.

Every precaution was taken to protect the command. Custer
and his staff marched at the head of the column followed by
the artillery. The long wagon train followed with its close-in
guard of infantry. On each flank of the wagon train were five
companies of cavalry, each flank command supplying a company of cavalry as rear guard on alternate days. No straggling
was permitted and no hunting was allowed except by special
permission or assignment.

In general the 60-day expedition went smoothly. There were
delays because of difficult terrain; the engineers had to provide
bridging and crossings at intervals at the periphery of the Hills.
In addition, the return to Fort Lincoln was very hot and parched,
causing considerable discomfort and the loss of a number of animals. Few Indians were seen and the one actual contact with
them occurred within the Hills when a small party of Sioux
camping there were surrounded by a cavalry detachment. A
Sioux brave attempted to seize a Santee scout's gun and during
the altercation the gun discharged, a bullet lodging in the
Sioux's groin. This was the only incident in which Indian blood
was spilled during the entire reconnaissance. On the homeward
march no Indians were seen, though some signs were observed.

Two cavalrymen died of dysentery and one was shot to death
in a quarrel. In other respects the health of the command remained high. Even those who were raw recruits when the command left Fort Lincoln agreed with the old veterans that it had
been a summer outing.

Though Custer had played down the discovery of gold in his
reports, it was touted to the heavens by the press. The frontier
newspapers, sensing an opportunity to build their communities
and their own profits, wrote rapturous accounts of "glittering
treasure," "gold in the grass roots," and of "color" that could be
found in any creek or stream.

The gold rush that followed the return of the Custer Expedition is not a part of this story. In brief it should be said that
prospectors organized and entered the Hills in groups. General
Sheridan had issued a warning that all trespassers would be arrested for their illegal entry. The Seventh Cavalry was employed
in this police work, turning over all such culprits to the civil authorities. The civil courts immediately released them. This illegal occupation of the Hills by prospectors was the final act in a

series of incidents leading up to a confrontation at the Little Big Horn in 1876.

S eldom does any man have the opportunity to accompany an expedition charged with penetrating and mapping an area hitherto unexplored by white men. Lieutenant James Calhoun had that opportunity when he was directed to accompany Lieutenant Colonel George Armstrong Custer on his 1874 military reconnaissance of the Black Hills. Calhoun—the author of the journal that follows—as Custer's acting assistant adjutant general during the reconnaissance, had charge of all official correspondence and the daily log. As a brother-in-law and intimate of the commanding officer of the expedition (if any person other than Custer's wife Libbie and his brothers Tom and Boston could be considered intimates) he was in a position to know all that unofficially transpired.

We are fortunate that Calhoun kept a copy of the daily log for himself and that he added to it his observations and comments. And we are more than fortunate that the Custer family preserved this unusual journal and that its owner, Colonel George Armstrong Custer III (United States Army, retired) has permitted us to reproduce it. Originally it had been preserved by General Custer's widow, Libbie. She left it to her husband's nearest living male descendant—Colonel Brice C. W. Custer, a grandson of General Custer's brother Nevin. In a search through his files for material to be used in my *General Custer's Libbie* (Superior Publishing Company, Seattle, Washington, 1976), I discovered this diary.

Brice Custer had been under the impression that the diary was one kept by his great-uncle; familiar as I was with General Custer's handwriting, it was obvious to me that he was not its author. Calhoun's handwriting is distinctive; a comparison of his handwriting with General Custer's cramped style was decisive. Careful reading of the diary's contents provided additional proof that no one but Lieutenant Calhoun could have written it.

In 1971 the Calhoun diary was transferred to Brice Custer's oldest son, Colonel George Armstrong Custer III (United States Army, retired), who has kindly permitted us to reproduce it.

James Calhoun was born in Cincinnati, Ohio, August 24, 1845, the son of a merchant. He had a brother, Frederick, who was two years his junior, and a younger sister, Charlotte. Since the Calhouns were a family of more than moderate means, young Jim was offered the opportunity of an education at the Mount Pleasant Military Academy at Sing Sing, New York, graduating on June 30, 1860.[25]

On January 7, 1865, at the age of nineteen, he enlisted in New York City in the Fourteenth United States Infantry. The three-year enlistment was credited to Groton, Tompkins County, New York. He gave his occupation as that of a clerk, and was described as being five feet eleven inches tall and as having brown eyes, light hair, and a fair complexion.[26]

The Fourteenth Infantry was ordered to Elmira, New York, until March, 1865, and was then transferred to the field, arriving at City Point, Virginia, on April 14. The company was assigned to provost duty until May, when it moved to Richmond, Virginia.[27]

On February 1, 1865, Calhoun was appointed a first sergeant of the Fourteenth Infantry, a rank he retained continuously until May 27, 1867. Obviously feeling he was qualified, on May 8, 1865, he appeared before a board of officers convening at Annapolis, Maryland, to consider noncommissioned officers of the regular army for promotion. Calhoun was considered by the board unqualified to be a commissioned officer.

The Fourteenth Infantry was expanded and became the Twenty-third Infantry. Two years after his first petition, Calhoun, a first sergeant of the Twenty-third Infantry's Company D, was again examined by a board that convened on May 27, 1867, at Camp Warner, Oregon. The board, composed of officers of the Twenty-third Infantry, found Calhoun proficient in spelling, reading, writing, composition, rhetoric, arithmetic, algebra, geometry, history, natural and mental philosophy, sketching, infantry tactics, army regulations, Articles of War, company accounts, and papers. It was recommended to the United States

25. Greta A. Cornell, "Mount Pleasant Academy 1814–1925," *The Westchester Historian* (Tuckahoe, N.Y.) 21(Spring 1956): 35–41; Daniel French, "Mount Pleasant Academy," *Historial and Statistical Gazeteer of New York State* (Syracuse, N.Y.: R. P. Smith, 1860), pp. 744–755; *Records of the Office of Adjutant General*, Records Group No. 94, Regular Army Enlistment Papers, National Archives, Washington, D.C.

26. *Records of the Office of Adjutant General*, Records Group No. 94.

27. Frederick H. Dyer, *A Compendium of the War of the Rebellion*, 3 vols. (New York: Thomas Yoseloff, reprinted 1959), 3:13–14, 17.

War Department that he be promoted to the rank of second lieutenant.[28]

Calhoun accepted his appointment as a second lieutenant in the Thirty-second Infantry on October 1, 1867, the appointment being dated July 31, 1867.[29] He officially joined the Thirty-second Infantry in December 1868, and he served at Camp Grant, Arizona Territory, and in the field until July 1869. Transferred to the Twenty-first Infantry, he served with that unit in Arizona until February 1870, when he obtained a leave of absence until October 1870. At that time he was unassigned, and was regarded as a supernumerary.

Three months later on January 1, 1871, he was assigned to the Seventh United States Cavalry, and on January 9 he was promoted to first lieutenant and was ordered to Bagdad, Kentucky.

Just prior to Calhoun's assignment to the Seventh Cavalry, Colonel George Stoneman, commanding officer of the Twenty-first Infantry stationed at Prescott, Arizona Territory, charged Calhoun with "rascality." In question was the disposal of about eighty tons of damaged surplus hay Calhoun considered unfit for public animals and for which he had been responsible as acting assistant quartermaster. The hay was valued at twenty-five dollars in gold coin per ton. Stoneman recommended that Calhoun be discharged from the service and that one year of pay be withheld until a certain amount of the hay was accounted for.

The allegation and charge were forwarded to Adjutant General E. E. Townsend, who referred the case to a board of officers that was to convene in Washington in December 1870.

In one of Calhoun's interrogatories, Calhoun questioned Lieutenant Colonel George Armstrong Custer (by deposition, Custer then being stationed at Fort Leavenworth, Kansas) as to the length of time they had known each other. Custer stated that he had known Calhoun very intimately for one year, though they had never served together; Custer then went on to say:

Officers who have served with him, in whose opinion I have every confidence, have spoken of him in very flattering terms. I feel con-

---

28. *Records of the Office of Adjutant General,* Records Group No. 94.

29. *Official Army Register for 1867* (Washington, D.C.: n.p., 1867), p. 80; *Widow's Pension Record,* Record of Maggie E. Calhoun, National Archives, Washington, D.C.

fident to speak of his general character as an officer and a gentleman. I regard him as one of the most promising officers of his grade, strictly honorable and possessed of far above average abilities of officers of his rank.

This testimony is given after a thorough understanding of, and inquiry into, the circumstances upon which the allegations against him are based. So high is the opinion of him entertained by the officers of my regiment that his transfer to that regiment has been asked for by Col. Sturgis, the Commanding Officer, and more than one Captain or Commanding Officer of companies has asked that he might be assigned to their company in the event of his transfer.[30]

First Lieutenant W. H. Winters, who knew Calhoun for three years and had served with him in Arizona near Tucson, gave a similar recommendation as to his reputation as an officer and gentleman.

Major John Green of the First Cavalry, commanding officer at Camp Thomas, Arizona Territory, stated that he had known Calhoun one year and regarded him as a "very good officer" with whom he was satisfied. Green testified that when he had received complaints from his officers that the corn fodder was unfit to feed their horses, Green spoke to Calhoun, who informed him that the fodder was surplus. Green told Calhoun to feed it to the cattle, who would at least eat part of it, so all of the fodder would not be wasted.

A board of survey convened at Camp Grant on March 10, 1870, to determine responsibility for the eighty tons of hay. Calhoun said Green had verbally directed him "not to receive any sorghum fodder but to accept all the corn fodder offered." Green countered that he had ordered Calhoun "not to receive more corn fodder than could be consumed each day." During Green's absence, Calhoun accepted between fifty and seventy-five tons of corn fodder which, though well stacked, spoiled because of internal heat.

The quartermaster general, Brigadier General Montgomery C. Meigs, upon receiving the report of the board of survey, remarked that hay was not sorghum fodder, nor was it corn fodder. He requested that proper names be used and that a tighter method of keeping accounts be employed. He said the practice of depending on a surplus was wrong. Meigs ordered three-

---

30. *Records of the Office of Adjutant General,* Records Group No. 94.

fourths of Calhoun's monthly pay stopped until his indebtedness to the United States was made good at the contract price of twenty-five dollars in gold coin per ton.

The quartermaster general wrote to General Custer on December 20, 1870, that he did not think that "Lieut. Calhoun's integrity was called in question or that he derived any pecuniary advantage from the transaction."

The board, presided over by Major General W. S. Hancock, concluded that Calhoun was "not unfit for the service."[31]

On November 27, 1871, Lieutenant Colonel George Crook dissolved a court of inquiry "investigating the circumstances leading to the stoppage of pay of First Lieutenant James Calhoun" and approved its findings "that they concur in the opinion of the General of the Army that the stoppage of the pay against Lt. Calhoun was unjust." A January 27, 1872, order from Adjutant General Townsend removed the stoppage of Calhoun's pay and ordered a refund of the amount that had already been removed.[32]

On March 7, 1872, James Calhoun married Custer's sister Margaret in the Methodist Church in Monroe; the Reverend James Venning officiated. Witnesses were the bride's brother Tom and the groom's sister Lottie, while General Custer and his wife, Libbie, stood proudly by. As further evidence of confidence in Calhoun's character and ability, Custer had him assume duties as his acting assistant adjutant general. In this capacity he served during Colonel David Stanley's expedition with the Seventh Cavalry as an escort for the Northern Pacific Railroad's surveying party, in which Custer acted as chief of cavalry under Stanley. During the 1874 reconnaissance of the Black Hills, Calhoun continued to serve under Custer in the same capacity.

In addition to years of military experience, much of which was in the West, Calhoun had traveled and seen more than most men his age. He had traveled extensively in Europe and America, being provided with more than an average opportunity to compare and analyze his experiences and observations. In describing the pleasure of preparing for a summer in the

---

31. Ibid.

32. Ibid.

field after a confining garrison life at a snowbound post, he observed that two-thirds of the men in the command were foreigners.

Of particular and revealing interest are his views as a white man entering for the first time a forbidden, impenetrable area that previous exploring parties had marched around. Previous parties had not attempted to explore the area because the repelling aspect of the hills from a distance gave the impression that in any further advance inward they would encounter greater obstacles.

Calhoun noted that the correspondents believed the Black Hills to be "a land of ambrosial luxury—flowing with milk and honey"; he cited reports that the hills contained vast treasures of immense wealth. The reactions of the several citizens accompanying the expedition drew his attention. For them he expressed some alarm: they rode at a considerable distance from the main column, which reminded him of the deaths of two men the previous summer (1873). That summer Dr. Honzinger, the veterinarian, and John Baliran, the sutler, were picked off and killed by Sioux Indians because they had tagged behind at too great a distance to be given any assistance when attacked.

During the early part of the expedition, while at the very periphery of the Hills, Calhoun concurred with several citizens who thought that the country had nothing inviting to offer and that it would be sinful to encourage immigration into and settlement of the area. But within the Hills his views changed; perhaps he compared the lush valleys of the Black Hills to the fertile Ohio River Valley of his childhood. He could recall the grasslands of Kentucky just across from his old home in Cincinnati, but even the blue grass of Kentucky couldn't compare. Now he was certain that Manifest Destiny would assert itself. What "a great pity," he wrote, "that this rich country should remain a wild state, uncultivated and uninhabited by civilized men." He was certain that "civilization will ere long throw heathen barbarism into oblivion . . . . Christian temples will elevate their lofty spires upward towards the azure sky while places of heathen mythology will sink to rise no more. This will be a period of true happiness."

Lieutenant James Calhoun didn't live long enough to see whether his prophecy came true. Two years later on June 25, 1876, he died with Custer in the Seventh Cavalry's disastrous defeat on the Little Big Horn. His body, in company with bodies of brother officers who died with him (Captain Tom Custer, Captain George Yates, and Lieutenant Algernon Smith), was reinterred at Fort Leavenworth National Cemetery in August 1877.

The Diary of Lieutenant James Calhoun

1874

June 14

Company G, 17th Infantry, under command of Captain Sanger arrived. Went into camp near Little Heart River.

June 16

Company I, 20th Infantry, under command of Captain Wheaton arrived.

June 17

Company I, 20th Infantry, left Fort Lincoln to join Company G, 17th Infantry at its camp near Little Heart River. Both these companies accompany the proposed expedition to the Black Hills.

June 18

Everybody is busy. Everything is alive. The sanguine expectation of leaving quarters, inspections, and unmitigated fatigues of a Post, for the more delightful atmosphere of nature is not only a boon to be desired, but an event of true pleasure too fully demonstrated in every countenance. Those unaccustomed to military life little know the pleasure it affords a soldier—especially a cavalryman—to be cut loose from garrison life, with its many crosses, anxieties and countless vexations—to be set free from a little strict discipline, from red tape and its high toned formalities—is a hyperbole of transcendant enjoyment, fully appreciated only by those whose lot is to compose the individual and collective part of the "regular army."

I am fully aware, there are a great many of our citizens and friends who reside in the states—entertain very erroneous ideas regarding the army. It is true that they speak from a conscientious standpoint—viz "honest conviction." But they speak from hearsay, from the press, from total ignorance of observation, or from a lack of correct testimony. I have heard persons say that a soldier's life was an idle one. That men joined the army to escape manual labor. That to an indolent person it was a portal of ease.

It is a great pity some of our citizen friends were not here in our midst—say today—to behold the amount of labor performed by the troops.

It is very fine, remarkably so, for men residing in densely populated cities, surrounded by every comfort, with no anxiety or care, who can lay on their easy beds of down, and fondly dream of a bright antepast—to pronounce judgement on the material of the army.

Is it not also a burning shame, that some men who frame and make the laws of the nation, should be guilty of making long harranges, and giving publicity to statements known to be fabulous if not true?

These men are constantly picking and scratching at the army. Retrenchment is their cry.

But persons living in glass houses "should not throw stones."

What would our progenitors think could it be possible for them to give utterance to thoughts in this our day and generation. Methinks they would stand on the highest pinnacle of the capitol and shout aloud—Away with you! Away with you! You are "weighed in the balances and found wanting."

And is it not well known that some of these men (our would-be enemies) are found to be among those who have amassed colossal fortunes from success achieved in financial schemes that have retarded—if not ruined—the commercial prosperity of this free country. Not satisfied with ill-gotten wealth, under the garb of "honest Statesmen"—with a hypocritical notion of reducing taxations, they turn their attention to the army.

They begrudge the hard earned pittance received by the officer and private soldier—and if not checked and bridled down by sensible, intelligent and upright men they would lop off the very best branches that hang with the choicest of fruit, on our noble tree.

There are officers and men in the service of the government (who have selected the army from choice, the same as any other profession) who are known to reflect credit upon the uniform they wear. Bright stars in the firmament of the military hemisphere.

Upright, intelligent and honest men, disdaining the very thought of wrong, and who ask from the government only that which is their rightful due—a fair and just compensation for faithful services rendered.

The progeny of our well-tried Officers cannot boast like the nobles of Europe of hereditary wealth, handed down with blood-stained hands from noble ancestors. Nor can they fold their arms with complacency, and boast like some of our young American bloods, that their patrimony came out of the coffers of the peoples' treasury—the bone and sinew of the nation.

NO—on the contrary—in the first place they have no extensive possessions—and in the second place blessed with talents "intelligence and good common sense" they are content to grapple with the world and its many vicissitudes to make headway for themselves.

ground to be occupied by the different companies, the sergeants were dismissed.

At noon today the six companies of cavalry stationed at this point rode out of the garrison fully armed and equipped. It was a lovely sight. To do justice to the occasion, General Custer took the head of the column. In my humble opinion the General does not look so well as he did when he marched his command through the streets of Yankton—some persons may differ with me—my finite conception of outward appearances may be very shallow. Nevertheless I claim a right to my opinion.

He is minus of the beautiful curly and long hair which used to hang gracefully down his shoulders. I may possibly create a smile but somehow or other I cannot help thinking of Sampson, how when he lost his hair, he became reduced in strength, and could not move the pillars of the temple. But faith

> Which laughs at impossibilities
> And cries—"it shall be done"

tells me that if the aborigines of the territories will allow the General a special favor he will move the pillars of their wigwams, and shake the very foundations of their villages. In lieu of using the jawbone of an ass to slay his enemies, he will try the effect of leaden pills, compounded by military chemists at our arsenals, which if taken in doses according to the nature of the disease will cleanse the blood, clear the head, and work a rapid and effectual cure.

As the command passed in front of the Officers' quarters, I took prominent position for the purpose of taking a few items of interest. The ladies came out on the porches, some appearing in groups, and here and there I could see the waving of handkerchiefs. Oh! what a thrilling scene. Here was scope for a wide continent of thought.

Who can disclose the many thoughts that passed through these feminine minds? Ah! there is a tender spot in every human breast. There are moments in our lives when the feelings of our inmost souls give way, and rush forth like the angry waters of a deluge, rising and overflowing everywhere. It would be sinful to stop the fountain or outlet by which the human heart obtains relief. Looking at the weeping willow we are constrained to admire its melancholy but lovely appearance, and acknowledge the many bright emblems contained in its downward, submissive and humble teachings. But does the willow not remind you of our friends in grief "bending its face in tears." Some of the Officers' ladies laughed heartily as they waved their handkerchiefs, but could you see inside the chambers of the soul, you would there find an aching void which the world can never fill.

Parting with the ties of nature (even for a short period) causes suffering and sorrow.

It is very reasonable that these ladies should entertain sanguinary thoughts regarding the future. For those who are dear and near to them, to travel through an unknown country known to be infested by Indians more or less hostile, is no imaginary cause of anxiety.

The Officers have similar feelings. Though belonging to the sterner sex they have feelings which can, and are touched, but it is well-known they are suppressed to a great extent by the many activities of a military life. But in the quiet hours of the night the work of contemplation begins. Half slumbering the machinery of the brain turns its attention to fond objects at a distance, and imagination lends itself to domestic and future happiness or woe.

The men as they rode by seemed in very good spirits. They looked remarkably well. In fact a healthier body of troops could not be found.

I have seen large bodies of troops in foreign countries on the march and in garrison, but I must candidly and honestly assert that for energy, bravery, and general appearance, American troops are far superior—in fact they take the premium. I am told, *and believe* that two-thirds of the American army is composed of foreigners. Foreigners as a general rule become initiated into the habits and customs of Americans pretty quick. The best remark that can be offered regarding our army is that the major portion are young men capable of sustaining any amount of hardship and fatigue imposed upon them.

European troops on the whole are cleaner and better posted in drills. This can be attributed to the fact, that in Europe every place is thickly settled. There are no expeditions to explore unknown countries. No settlements to protect from harm. No new posts to build, to pave the way for civilization. Having no unusual manual labor to perform, they have time to make soldiering strictly a profession.

Having arrived at camp or the place chose for a camp, the men dismount and picket their horses with lariats, taking care to secure them with side lines. Then pitching their tents and arranging everything in order, the place has the appearance to all intents and purposes of a camp.

Many a good old yarn is told around a camp fire. The soldiers when not on duty generally sit on the ground, and indulge in a puff of the luxurious weed. They recount former adventures, and post the recruits regarding Indian warfare. I have listened to many a side splitting joke, and found these men conversant with frontier life.

Many a thrilling incident is told, and could you hear some of our soldiers (especially those members of the 7th Cavalry who served in the Department of the Missouri) tell of their many hardships, and hair breadth escapes, I am sure you would listen with anxiety and attention.

The following order was issued at a late hour in the day.

Headquarters Black Hills Expedition
Fort Abraham Lincoln, D. T.
June 20th, 1874

General Orders

No. 1

I. In accordance with par. I, Special Orders No. 117, from Headquarters Department of Dakota dated St. Paul, Minn. June 8th, 1874; the undersigned hereby assume command of the forces, composing the Black Hills Expedition.

II. The following appointments on the staff of the Commdg. Officer are hereby made, and published for the information of all concerned.

Acting Aid
   Lieut. Col. Fred D. Grant, A.D.C. to the Lieut. General.
Acting Assistant Adjutant General
   1st Lieut. James Calhoun, 7th Cavalry.
Quartermaster and Commissary
   1st Lieut. A. E. Smith, 7th Cavalry.

Chief Medical Officer
    Assistant Surgeon J. W. Williams, U.S.A.
Engineer Officer
    Captain William Ludlow, Corps of Engineer.

June 21

The four (4) companies of the 7th Cavalry, stationed at Fort Rice under command of Captn. V. K. Hart, 7th Cavy., arrived at noon today.

Private T. A. Hersfield, Co. G. 7th Cavy., was accidentally drowned whilst watering his horse. General G. A. Forsyth, Col. F. D. Grant, Col. Ludlow and a detachment of engineers arrived this P.M.

June 22

The following named citizens, accompany the Expedition;
Professor [Newton H.] Winchell Geologist

Professor [A. B.] Donaldson	Assistant Geologist
Mr. [George Bird] Grinnell	Geologist and one Assistant
Mr. [W. H.] Woods	Assistant Engineer
Mr. [William H.] Illingworth	Photographer
Mr. [Samuel J.] Barrows	Correspondent, N. Y. *Tribune*
Mr. [William Eleroy] Curtis	Correspondent, Chicago *Inter-Ocean*
Mr. [Fred W.] Powers	Correspondent, St. Paul *Press*
Mr. [A. B.] Donaldson	Correspondent, St. Paul *Pioneer*
Mr. [Nathan H.] Knappen	Correspondent, Bismarck *Tribune*

Thermometer stood at 108° in the shade at noon today.

June 23

To give the reader a full detail, I had better descend into the particulars of this proposed Expedition. I am somewhat ignorant of most of the facts, and wish to be understood in that light.

The Commanding Officer of the Expedition has expressed a desire on many occasions to explore the Black Hills, believing that it would open a rich vein of wealth calculated to increase the commercial prosperity of this country. Having this object in view, he made known his impressions through the recognized military channels—which were favorably received, and transmitted to the proper quarter for consideration—the result of which has received the hearty approval of the government. Generals Sheridan and Terry have warmly endorsed the propriety of an expedition to the Black Hills. From the first they have rendered all the aid possible.

I see from a telegram from Department Headq'rs dated St. Paul, Minn., June 22nd, 1874, that the Commanding General wishes the Expedition Commander to delay his command for a few days in order that the new Springfield carbines recently adopted by the government may be furnished the several companies of the 7th Cavalry and to make it more binding states that he *"especially wants this command armed with the new carbines."*

The press has praised the Black Hill country to the skies. We are informed in glowing terms "that it is believed to be, a land of ambrosial luxury—flowing with milk and honey." In fact so much has been circulated regarding this section of country, that thousands are wild with curiosity—longing to see it. The excitement in the western settlements is so intense, that if the government does not take the matter in hand, the settlers will penetrate into this country on their own responsibility.

It is supposed in the vicinity of the Black Hills there are vast treasures of immense wealth. That rich mines await the industry of the hard-working miner. That precious metals invite discovery, and that in the bottoms of the many streams, and other parts of this domain, large deposits of gold are to be found.

There must be some truth in the many reports regarding this country or the Indians would not hold such a sacred claim to it. It is well-known that Indians have a great superstition concerning this place.

They believe that the "Great Spirit" will suffer no pale face to inhabit it. I have read in a newspaper of an Indian squaw going into one of our forts some years ago (I believe it was Fort Laramie) and offering to barter or sell a lump of gold about the size of an egg, which she said was obtained from the Black Hills.

Adventurers in small parties and expeditions have from time to time left the western settlements for the purpose of visiting this place, but have either failed to return and report results, or

10

from embarrassments and difficulties placed in their path returned disheartened without reaching their destination.

An expedition consisting of quite a number of citizens left Bozeman, M. T. early this spring, fully determined to penetrate into the Black Hills. They were well armed and equipped, and fully expected to surmount every difficulty which presented itself. Alas! they did not weigh *this* and *that* together. Building castles in the air they predicted a bright hereafter. Leaving the goal of operations, with great expectations, they marched through the Indian country, forgetting that the stanchion of success depended upon numbers, unity, and a practical knowledge of the art of war. Although accustomed to frontier life and Indian warfare, they overestimated their own strength and underestimated the strength of their foes. I would not for one moment question the bravery and stability of those men. They are made of the right metal, and are willing to suffer immolation to advance the cause of civilization. They should be applauded by a generous public, for the work they took in hand for indeed it was a plucky undertaking. But arriving at Tongue River, M. T. they were attacked by a numberless body of Indians who checked farther advancement of the Bozeman Expedition. A camisade made by the red forces crippled them to such an extent as to render further progress impracticable.[33] The strength of the hostile foe was so great that they were compelled to retreat and return to their homes.

General Custer, fully alive to the interests of the Northwest, wishes to see this country for himself, and if it be advantageous or worthy of future development, he will have the satisfaction of presenting an honest statement in a clear and proper light for the information of the whole world. This expedition is intended to be one of the best that ever moved west. Weighing this and that together it will defy all opposition. Though the propriety of this movement has been questioned by some, and critics have more or less condemned it, yet the Expedition will move under the auspices of the Government.

This expedition is a peaceful one, and will enter into no hostilities without a cause. Perhaps some of our eminent divines who

---

33. A *camisade* is a surprise attack conducted at night.

11

have preached so much of late regarding the treaty of '68 might send a gospel message to some hostile chiefs with a view of making both ends meet.

The following is the roster of troops composing the forces of the Black Hills Expedition:

Lieut. Colonel G. A. Custer, 7th Cavalry.
Major G. A. Forsyth, 9th Cavalry.
Major J. G. Tilford, 7th Cavalry.
Lieut. Col. F. D. Grant, A. D. C. to Lt. General.
Capt. Wm. Ludlow, Engineer Corps, U. S. A.
1st Lieut. James Calhoun, 7th Cavy., A. A. A. G.
1st Lieut. A. E. Smith, 7th Cavy., A. A. Q. M. & A. C. S.
Asst. Surgeon J. W. Williams, U. S. A., Chief Medical Officer
Actg. Asst. Surgeon S. J. Allen, U. S. A.
Actg. Asst. Surgeon A. C. Bergen, U. S. A.

Artillery Detachment	1st Lieut. Josiah Chance, 17 Infy.
Detachment & Indian Scouts.	2nd Lieut. G. D. Wallace, 7th Cavy.
Company A, 7th Cavalry	Capt. Myles Moylan, 7th Cavy. 2nd Lieut. C. A. Varnum, 7th Cavy.
Company B, 7th Cavalry	2nd Lieut. B. H. Hodgson, 7th Cavy.
Company E, 7th Cavalry	1st Lieut. Thos. M. McDougall
Company F, 7th Cavalry	Captain G. W. Yates, 7th Cavy.
Company G, 7th Cavalry	1st Lieut. D. McIntosh, 7th Cavy.
Company L, 7th Cavalry	1st Lieut. Thos. W. Custer, 7th Cavy.
Company C, 7th Cavalry	Capt. V. K. Hart, 7th Cavy. 2nd Lieut. H. M. Harrington, 7th Cavy.
Company H, 7th Cavalry	Capt. F. W. Benteen, 7th Cavy. 1st Lieut. F. M. Gibson, 7th Cavy.
Company K, 7th Cavalry	Capt. Owen Hale, 7th Cavy. 1st Lieut. E. S. Godfrey, 7th Cavy.

Company M, 7th Cavalry	Capt. T. H. French, 7th Cavy.
	1st Lieut. E. G. Mathey,
	7th Cavy.
Company G, 17th Infantry	Capt. L. H. Sanger, 17th Infy.
	2nd Lt. Geo. H. Roach,
	17th Infy.
Company I, 20th Infantry	Capt. Lloyd Wheaton,
	20th Infy.
	2nd Lt. J. G. Gates, [20th Infy.]

The following orders were issued today, for the information of the Command:

Headq'rs. Black Hills Expedition
Fort A. Lincoln, D. T.
June 23rd, 1874

Special Orders

No. 9   "Extract"

I. Major George A. Forsyth, 9th Cavalry, A. D. C. to the Lieut. General, having complied with par. I, Special Orders No. 41 from Headq'rs Military Division of the Missouri, directing him to join this expedition is hereby assigned to duty with that portion of the 7th Cavalry accompanying the Expedition.

By order of Brevet Major General Custer

(s'd)   James Calhoun
1st Lieut. 7th Cavalry
A. A. A. General.

*

Headq'rs Black Hills Expedition
Fort A. Lincoln, D. T.
June 23rd, 1874

Circular

No. 11

Company Commanders are hereby notified that the Brevet Major General commanding is in receipt of an official telegram from Department Headquarters informing him that Springfield carbines Cal. 45 have been ordered for this command. This will necessitate a change in the waist belts already prepared to carry cartridges of 50 calibre. All

Springfield muskets, and the various patterns of carbines now in the hands of the men belonging to the cavalry companies of this post, will be stored at this post, until the return of the expedition.

By order of Brevet Major General Custer

> s'd   James Calhoun
> 1st Lieut., 7th Cavalry
> Act. Asst. Adjutant General.

*

June 30

The following orders were issued today.

> Headquarters Black Hills Expedition
> Fort A. Lincoln, D. T.
> June 30th, 1874

Circular

No. 12

Company Commanders will carry five day's rations in their Company Wagons, commencing on the 1st and ending the 5th proximo. Ration returns will be sent to this office in the morning for approval.

By order of Brevet Maj. Gen'l Custer

> s'd   James Calhoun
> 1st Lieut., 7th Cavalry
> A. A. A. G.

*

> Headq'rs Black Hills Expedition
> Fort A. Lincoln, D. T.
> June 30th, 1874

Circular

No. 13

Company Commanders are hereby informed that the arms, ammunition, and other stores required for the command will arrive tonight, and all necessary issues will be made as early as practicable tomorrow.[34]

By order of Brevet Major General Custer

(s'd) James Calhoun
1st Lieut., 7th Cavalry
A. A. A. G.

*

Headq'rs Black Hills Expedition
Fort A. Lincoln, D. T.
June 30th, 1874

General Orders

No. 3

The following order of march will be observed.

1st. The Detachment of Indian Scouts, Lieut. Geo. D. Wallace, 7th Cavalry Commdg.

2nd. The Battery of Gatling Guns, Lieut. Josiah Chance, 17th Infy. Commdg.

3rd. The ambulance and wagon trains, the latter when practicable to move in four columns, the ambulances preceding the latter, company wagons to be formed in the outer columns in the order occupied by the respective companies. The pioneer wagon being in advance of one of the columns.[35]

4th. The Infantry Battalion in two columns, Captain L. H. Sanger, 17th Infy. Commanding. The commdg. Officer Infantry Battn. will regulate the distance within three hundred yards at which his command will follow the train.

5th. One company of the 7th Cavalry as rear guard to be designated as hereafter specified. The right Battalion, 7th Cavy., Major George A. Forsyth, 9th Cavalry commdg., will habitually march on the right flank, and opposite the center of the train and at such distance not exceeding four hundred yards as the Battalion Commander may direct.

---

34. *Bismarck Tribune*, 1 July 1876.

35. The pioneer corps cut down trees, dug away hillsides, bridged streams, and made roads for the advancing column. Companies were alternated for this arduous and important task.

The left Battalion, 7th Cavalry, Major J. G. Tilford, 7th Cavy., commdg., will habitually march on the left flank and opposite the centre of the train, and at such distance not exceeding four hundred yards as the Battalion Commander may direct. Each commanding officer of a cavalry battalion will cause flanking parties consisting of a non-commissioned officer and three men from each company to move opposite and to the right of their respective companies and at such distance from the latter as will most readily enable the flankers to give timely notice of the approach or presence of an enemy without unnecessary exposure of the flankers. The latter should not pass beyond the view or the range of the carbines of their respective companies.

Each commander of a cavalry battalion will consider the entire flank upon which his command is moving as under the special protection of the latter, and will hold his command in constant readiness while on the march or in camp to repel without further orders any attack directed against his particular flank. of the main command. The Commdg. Officer of the Infantry Battalion will consider the train generally as under the protection of his command, and in addition will while on the march be in readiness to render support to the rearguard should the latter be pressed or suddenly assulted by a hostile force. Lieut. Wallace commanding Indian Scouts will detail daily from his command ten (10) scouts as the advance of the advanced guard. This advance will be instructed to precede the column keeping within a thousand yards as well as within sight of the latter. He will also send such special scouting parties to prominent points near the line of march, as the Commanding Officer of the Expedition may direct from time to time.

Line Officers will not leave their respective commands without special permission to that effect from their Battalion Commander. The Commdg. officers of the Battery and Detachment of Indian Scouts will habitually march at the head of their respective commands. The Acting Quartermaster Sergeants of companies are authorized to march with their respective company wagons, all other enlisted men on duty with their companies will march with the latter.

The non-commiss'd staff, band, and other enlisted men on duty at these Headq'rs will march under the command of the Acting Assistant Adjutant General near the head of the column.[36]

---

36. Grinnell observed that a band of sixteen men on white horses played "Garry Owen" as the column left Fort Lincoln. Grinnell called it a novel experience to start into hostile Indian country singing; to the soldiers it was exhilarating. The Seventh Cavalry's Field Return of that period indicated there were only fifteen men in the band. See George Bird Grinnell, *Two Great Scouts* (Cleveland: Arthur H. Clark Co., 1928), p. 240.

Lieut. A. E. Smith, 7th Cavy., Quartermaster of the Expedition, will habitually march at the head of his train; he will also, as Commissary of Subsistence, require the beef herd which accompanies the Expedition to be driven opposite and near to the train.

The following assignments of medical officers are hereby made upon the recommendation of the Chief Medical Officer of the Expedition. Ass't Surgeon J. W. Williams, U. S. A. in addition to his duties as Chief Medical Officer of the Expedition is assigned to duty with the right Battalion of the 7th Cavy.

Acting Asst. Surgeon S. J. Allen, U. S. A. is assigned to duty with the left Battalion 7th Cavalry.

Acting Asst. Surgeon A. C. Bergen, U. S. A. is assigned to duty with the Infantry Battalion.

The medical officers herein named will habitually march with the battalions to which they are assigned and in camp will attend sick call and prescribe for the sick of their respective battalions. The Chief Medical Officer of the Expedition will however give a general supervision to the medical duties required in battalions other than that to which he is herein specially assigned.

He will also provide medical attendance and treatment for such cases of sickness as may require attention among the officers and men at these Headquarters, and for the civil employees, accompanying the Expedition.

The general plan of camp will be that adopted in the present camp. The Infantry Battalion being advanced far enough from the nearest flanks of the two cavalry battalions to allow the wagon train to be parked in its rear and connecting the flanks of the right and left Battalions of cavalry.

Each cavalry company will occupy a front of fifty paces; the picket line will be stretched fifteen paces in front of the line of men's tents. All the latter will be on the company line except the tent authorized as a cook tent, and two shelter tents for the use of company cooks; those tents will be pitched inside the picket line, fifteen paces from the latter and near the company wagon.

Company Officers' tents will be pitched outside the line of men's tents, fifteen paces from and opposite the centre of the line. Officers' cook tents will be pitched fifteen paces in rear of the line of officers' tents, the latter to face their respective companies.

No tents will be allowed other than those authorized by existing orders.

As soon as the camp ground to be occupied by their respective commands has been indicated to Battalion Commanders, the latter will at once and before commencing preparation to go into camp throw out a strong line of pickets to occupy a commanding line opposite to, and several hundred yards, depending upon the nature of the ground from their respective camps.

The Commanding Officer of the "Detachment of Indian Scouts" will at same time post such pickets in advance as will cover that front.

The line of pickets about camp will be maintained until relieved by the picket guard at retreat. The latter under the personal direction of the Officer of the Day will be posted at retreat and relieved by Battalion Commanders immediately after reveille by details from their respective battalions.

As the utmost prudence will necessarily be maintained to prevent the surprise of individuals or of small parties by prowling Indians, no member of the command will go beyond the line of flankers while on the march, nor beyond the line of pickets while in camp except by special authority from the Commanding Officer of the Expedition, and then such parties will pass and repass the lines at the same point.

As a pistol or rifle shot will be the signal of danger, the discharge of fire arms within or near the lines by day or night is strictly prohibited.

Firing at game from the column or from the vicinity of camp is prohibited except under circumstances warranting special permission.

Hunting parties will only be organized under authority from these Headquarters.

No horse will be grazed in camp without being secured by side lines and lariats. All horses will be fastened to the picket line at retreat; vicious horses will have side lines attached to them to prevent injury to other horses. The stable guards will also be instructed to act as pickets, and properly given the alarm in case of attack. Commanders of cavalry battalions will in addition to the usual stable guard of three men and one non-commissioned officer require an additional force of at least four men from a company all under command of an officer to be posted in good position at least three hundred yards beyond the herd dismounted. The Quartermaster of the Expedition will cause the mule herd to be grazed under similar regulations as to lariats and will require one teamster to every fourth team, and one wagonmaster to be constantly with the mule herd while the latter is grazing. He will also see that the mule herd is grazed as near to camp as the condition of the grazing will permit.

As the object of this Expedition is a peaceable one, care will be taken not to molest or in any manner disturb any Indians who may be encountered on the march unless the latter should first act in a hostile manner. As a measure of precaution no party of Indians no matter how small will be permitted to approach the vicinity of the picket lines by day or night. Officers and men are particularly cautioned against being drawn into the trap usually laid by Indians by the latter exposing a small number and endeavoring to induce pursuit.

This command is about to march through a country infested by Indians more or less hostile and even should the latter as it is hoped, not engage in general warfare and the usual acts of hostilities, there is no doubt but that they will endeavor to make captures of stock and to massacre small parties found imprudently beyond the lines. To guard against this the utmost caution and prudence on the part of every member of this command will be required. While it is hoped that these admonitions will prove ample, the Commanding Officer of the Expedition will promptly apply correctives of the most summary character in all cases of violation of the orders contained herein.

Orders giving a list of trumpet calls will be published hereafter.

VI. While on the march reveille will be sounded at a quarter before three. The General will be sounded at a quarter past four, and the advance at 5 o'clock. The cavalry will not saddle up until the signal "Boots and Saddles" has been sounded from these Headquarters. Tents will be left standing until the "General" has sounded. There will be two general roll calls daily, reveille and retreat, at both of which the men will fall in under arms and the result of the roll calls be reported to the "Battalion Commanders."

In the case of the absence of officers from either roll call, the fact will be reported by the Battalion Commander to these Headquarters. The Commanding officers of Cavalry Battalions will give their personal attention to the proper performance of stable duty, and will require the presence of company officers during the performance of this duty.

By Command of Brevet Major General Custer.

James Calhoun
1st Lieut., 7th Cavalry
Act. Asst. Adjutant General

*

July 1

The new Springfield arms and ammunition were issued to the command today. They seem to give great satisfaction. In fact

19

this Expedition is so thoroughly equipped as to render it one of the most complete that ever moved west.

Orders have been given for the command to move at 8 o'clock in the morning. The men are exceedingly anxious to be under way.[37]

*

Headq'rs Black Hills Expedition
Fort Ab'rm Lincoln, D. T.
July 1st, 1874

Circular

No. 17

There will be carried in the company wagons two days forage to be fed the second and third day after leaving this point. Five days rations for the men will also be carried in the wagons.[38] One wall tent and three "A" tents will be carried in the company wagons, all other authorized canvass will be carried on the saddles.

By order of Brevet Major General Custer

James Calhoun
1st Lieut., 7th Cavalry
A. A. A. G.

*

July 2

The general sounded at 7 A.M., Boots & Saddles 7:50 A.M. To Horse 8 A.M. Advance 8:10 A.M.

It is a delightful morning. The air is serene and the sun is shining in all its glory. The birds are singing sweetly, warbling their

---

37. On the evening of July 1, Gordon J. Keeney, formerly of Erie, Michigan (ten miles south of Monroe), and then a resident of Fargo, Dakota Territory, visited the Custers to talk over old times in Michigan. Keeney, believing that the expedition would be fiercely contested and anticipating disaster for his old friend, lingered that evening until he missed the last boat to cross the Missouri River. A detail of soldiers rowed him across the river to Bismarck. *Fargo Forum*, June 4, 1950.

38. The bill of fare on escort duty consisted of coffee, bacon, and hard bread. Potatoes and onions, if available, were taken. An abundance of game provided variety to the diet.

sweet notes as they soar aloft. Nature seems to smile on our movement. Everything seems to encourage us onward.

Some of the ladies of the garrison came out to give us a parting cheer. Col. Thompson also came to bid adieu.

As we commenced our march westward the Band of the 7th Cavalry played the popular air "the girl I left behind me," music appropriate to the occasion.

The grazing on our route is very good. Battalion Commanders carried out to the letter the requirements of General Orders No. 3 mentioned heretofore.

Our immense wagon train under the direction of Capt. A. E. Smith, 7th Cavalry Quartermaster of the Expedition, moved at a rapid rate considering the immense amount of freight carried. Travelling over a rough prairie a wagon train often has to depart from the straight course, and thus make the distance longer.[39]

About 5 miles from our starting point we found a good supply of wholesome water, refreshing to man and beast.

The wagon train had several bad crossings which caused a delay of several hours. Four wagons sunk into the mire and had to be unloaded. The contents of one wagon had to be left on the prairie.

Several N. C. O. and privates belonging to the Infantry Battalion fell down from the effects of the oppressive heat and had to ride in the ambulances.

Saw a bright comet this evening. Wood obtained 2 miles from camp—not much water.

Arrived at Camp No. 2—marched 11 1/10 miles. On arriving at camp a horse ridden by Private Hiram E. Brown, Co. F, 7th Cavy. orderly for the commdg. officer, broke loose and went

---

39. Wood, water, and terrain regulated the length of each day's march. As General George Forsyth observed in his *Story of the Soldier* (New York: D. Appleton and Company, 1900), p. 163: "A day's march is commonly from water to water, and that may be anywhere from eight to 28 miles."

Custer, knowing his men and horses needed hardening and conditioning for the trek ahead, customarily started an expedition at a slow and relatively easy pace, lengthening each day of travel progressively if circumstances permitted.

back in the direction of Fort Lincoln. Private Brown with two Indian Scouts were ordered back to overtake and catch the horse if possible. The mail arrived by Indian Scouts from Lincoln.

July 3

Reveille sounded at 4 o'clock. The General at 7 o'clock—Boots and Saddles 7:45. To horse 7:55. The advance at 8 o'clock.

A detail of 5 men were sent at 4:30 this A.M. to load the freight which was left on the prairie yesterday.

The Indian Scouts were sent back with the mail.[40] This is a very hot day. Several soldiers taken sick from the effects of drinking too much water. There is no doubt but this is the best Expedition that ever moved west—The most improved pattern of arm, and an abundant supply of ammunition. This gives confidence to the officers and men.

Marched 14 144/1,000 [sic] miles, arrived at Camp No. 3; very little water, no wood. The grazing good and of the best quality.

July 4

Reveille 3:30. General 4:30. Boots and Saddles 4:55. To horse 5:05. Advance 5:10.

Early this morning General Custer's orderly returned with his horse. He brought a letter from Mrs. Custer. Lieut. E.G. Mathey, 7th Cavalry, and detachment who were sent on detached service several days before our departure from Fort Lincoln also arrived and joined the command. It is a cloudy morning, a delightful breeze and the cool air makes the march easy.

I noticed several citizens diverging from the command, and riding at a considerable distance from the main column. If they

---

40. Custer wrote to his wife, Libbie, that the heavily loaded wagons sank to the hubs the day before because recent rains had so softened the ground. He wanted her to know that Johnson, the new Negro cook, served hot biscuits and hotcakes that morning. With his letter he sent her a young curlew (a long-legged bird with a curved bill) as a playmate to the wild goose they had been caring for; Libbie was advised to feed it grasshoppers. Elizabeth B. Custer, *Boots and Saddles* (New York: Harper and Brothers, 1885), pp. 298–99.

would study the best means of safety they would stop this practice.

Travelling through an Indian Country it behooves all men to keep within the lines. If some of our lamented friends who were killed by hostile Indians near the Yellowstone and Tongue rivers last year had adopted proper precaution they would have been in the land of the living today. I observed that the Commanding Officer of the Expedition saw a newspaper correspondent guilty of indiscretion in this matter, and sent his Sergeant Major with an order that he wanted to see him. What took place in the way of conversation I do not know; but probably this gentleman may be thankful for the advice given him, for I presume he was informed of the risk he was running, by leaving the command.

It was amusing to see some of our Indian scouts thrown off their young ponies.[41]

At 8 o'clock today we crossed the trail of the Yellowstone Expedition which left Fort Rice in 1872. Arrived at Camp No. 4 at 10:45 A.M.; after having marched 13 miles. Camped on a beautiful creek. Very little wood, a beautiful clear stream of water.[42]

Portions of this stream is so deep as to admit of the men swimming and taking a good bath.

---

41. There are varying and conflicting reports as to the number of Indian scouts with the expedition. Correspondent William E. Curtis (*Chicago Inter-Ocean*, July 29, 1874) reported there were nearly one hundred scouts—forty Rees, fifty Santees, and a few Sioux. The July 8 issue of the *Bismarck Tribune* stated that twenty-five Santees would accompany the column. Private Theodore Ewert noted in his diary that there were thirty-nine Rees, seven Sioux, and twenty-nine Santees (a total of seventy-five scouts). The Field Return of the Expedition indicated there were only seventy-six Indian scouts. John M. Carroll and Lawrence A. Frost, eds., *Private Theodore Ewert's Diary of the Black Hills Expedition of 1874* (Piscataway, N.J.: Consultant Resources, Inc., 1976).

42. On July 4, 1874, a friend of Libbie's, Captain Alfred G. Bates of Monroe, led a successful charge of the Second Cavalry against a large encampment of hostile Arapahoes. Hugh Knoefel, editor of the *Northern Wyoming Daily News*, claims that the Second Cavalry's battlefield thirty-seven miles southeast of Worland was the site of Wyoming's bloodiest Fourth of July. Twenty-five hostiles, two soldiers, and two Shoshone allies were killed in the battle.

On that same day the *Army and Navy Journal* (July 4, 1874), in writing of the Black Hills Expedition, called Custer "that luckiest of all lucky leaders, whose prudent and successful conduct of the Yellowstone Expedition, sometimes since, brought him so many honors," then added that Custer's "luck will be found to consist largely in that mixture of daring and prudence that is sure to make its mark in any pursuit of life. . . . Custer is lucky, chiefly because he is always ready."

The pioneer party built a bridge over the creek this afternoon, and the Q'rmaster moved the train containing the Q'rmaster and Commissary Stores over in order to save unnecessary delay in the morning.[43]

July 5

We passed over a splendid country today, good grazing, the best of pasturage. Buffalo and grammar grasses as far as the eye can see. At the many halts our horses had every facility to eat of these nutritious grasses.

Several bad crossings. M Company, 7th Cavalry, being in advance, were detailed as the pioneer party, and worked faithfully, while the band played some lively airs.[44]

One teamster and a Q'rmasters mule badly hurt at one of the crossings.[45]

Arrived at Camp No. 5; marched 16 4/10 miles. A good supply of wood and water. An excellent camp suitable for all purposes. The stock have a bountiful supply of good grass to satisfy their hungry appetites.

July 6

Reville 2:45. General 4:10. Boots and Saddles 4:35. To Horse

---

43. *Chicago Inter-Ocean* (July 30, 1874) was of the opinion that "General Custer is a famous road maker, and to him, as to the great Napoleon, nothing is impossible." Custer's pioneer wagon was filled with spades, shovels, picks, axes, scythes, and other tools. Curtis observed that when the party reached a place that had to be bridged, Custer selected the spot and then assisted in the work. The extra wagon tongues each teamster carried were placed crosswise in two or three layers and then covered with brush, sod, and everything else the three or four hundred men could obtain. When the bridges were completed, the artillery and ambulances crossed first, followed by the six-mule teams.

44. Just before the expedition left Fort Lincoln, Custer's brother Boston (who served as the expedition's forage master) wrote to his cousin Emma Reed in Monroe that "the band plays every night and morning." (Boston Custer to Emma Reed, July 1, 1874, Colonel Brice C. W. Custer Collection.)

45. Private Theodore Ewert, acting as orderly trumpeter for Custer, entered into his diary that the teamster had urged his mules across a "bad creek," which resulted in the driver being thrown from his seat. The wagon wheels passing over his leg fractured the leg in two places; the leg was set immediately. Carroll and Frost, *Ewert's Diary*, p. 11.

4:55. Advance 5:00.

At roll call this A.M. Private Edward Stout, Co. B 7th Cavalry, was reported absent.

Abundance of game seen in every direction. I heard old frontiersmen (and many old soldiers too) say that the grass seen today was the best they ever saw on the prairie—rich grammar grass.

Bloody Knife, an Indian Scout, rode up to the Commanding Officer and pointing to the left motioned for permission to go in that direction, which was granted. In ten minutes he returned bearing something resembling a white flag with two bunches of tobacco tied to the same, which the Indian Scouts say is a token of peace.

As far as the eye can reach green fields of luxuriant grass are visible—just like a beautiful park.

Some of the soldiers were very careless in shooting across the column. Antelope were plentiful. Some came within 25 yards of the command, and the soldiers were firing in all directions. The excitement at one time became so great as to cause a stampede with one of the artillery carriages, and might have proven serious if prompt aid had not been rendered.[46] This caused a circular to be issued prohibiting shooting at game, unless where permission has been obtained from the Commanding Officer, and then far away from the column. One horse of Co. "K" 7th Cavy. bitten by a rattlesnake—Ammonia administered. General Custer killed two (2) antelope.

---

46. The fifth day was one of excitement, as Professor A. B. Donaldson reported to the *St. Paul Pioneer* on July 28, 1874. On that day Illingworth, the photographer, proved himself the Nimrod of the hunters, killing three antelope. At the time the antelope were seen so frequently that the men became excited and fired wildly from the ranks. At one point, Custer was about to fire at an antelope when several of the Indian scouts shot it. Custer promptly fired several shots over their heads as a reminder that they were trespassing; they quickly emptied their saddles, flattening themselves on the ground.

On another occasion, seven antelope led by a buck crossed in front of the column within fifteen feet of the soldiers. In spite of orders to the contrary the men fired volleys, but were only able to bring down the buck. The driver of a four-horse team drawing a Gatling gun "left his post for a moment to salute the herd with his six-shooter." His frightened team ran away with the Gatling gun, but fortunately the herd became bogged in a nearby slough. The only reprimand was an order that the driver remain dismounted for the remainder of that day.

Marched 12 7/10 miles, arrived at Camp No. 6. Camped on the N branch of the Cannonball River.[47]

The pioneer party were sent to build a bridge to enable the wagon train to cross in the morning.

July 7

The Command moved at sun up.

Dreary marching all day long, beneath a burning hot sun.

Several bad crossings—delayed several hours. Water was found about every six miles in quantities to suit our wants. Water on a hot day like this is very refreshing to man and beast.

Water, pure blessed water. There is nothing in this world that can quench the thirst like water. It is one of God's very best gifts to man. Those who have travelled through the sandy deserts of Asia tell a fearful tale regarding the awful pangs caused by thirst. Mungo Park in his writings has not forgotten to enlighten the public on this subject.

But those familiar with the broad plains of America can inform you that they have travelled over some portions thereof, at certain seasons of the year for several days without quenching their thirst, and know by experience the great suffering endured without water.

But so far the plains of Dakota have proven very good, both as regards water and grazing.

Two Badgers caught alive.

Arrived at Camp No. 7. Marched 30 4/10 miles, good grazing, very little wood, and abundant supply of water. Camped on a

---

47. The heat that day had been oppressive, averaging well over one hundred degrees. Ambulances were full of men who, overcome by the heat, had fallen along the route. The animals—horses, mules, and cattle—were affected by the heat even more. "Whenever the train stops," reported Curtis, "the air is hideous with the braying of the poor, thirsty, tired mules."

The finely powdered alkali dust that covered the land sifted its way through everything, painfully burning the skin and scalding the mucous membranes. The heat and wind parched and cracked the soldiers' lips and galled the sweating flesh of the cavalryman wherever his flesh touched his horse or saddle.

creek. I am informed by the Commd'g Officer that this is probably the South branch of the Cannonball River.

I would have remarked that while I praise this country for its super abundance of grazing and water, that I have to confess that is poor for wood or fuel of any description.[48]

The horse bitten by a rattlesnake is doing well.

July 8

Early this morning an alarm was given by one of the pickets firing off his piece. Fortunately it amounted to nothing.[49]

Private Edward Stout Company B 7th Cavalry, mentioned July 6th as being absent, reported this morning. He says that being under the influence of liquor he went into the shade and fell fast asleep, and awoke after the command had left. He was about to come out of ambush when he discovered a number of Indians looking around the old camping place picking up what they could find, and being an old soldier and accustomed to similar adventures out West, he concluded to wait until the cover of night should afford an opportunity of travelling without being discovered.

The Command did not move until 7:30 o'clock as a bridge had to be constructed to allow the wagon train to cross over.

General Custer killed one antelope, and also obtained three prairie owls and one eagle.

---

48. Donaldson advised *St. Paul Pioneer* readers in the July 7 issue that to advance six miles over the extremely hilly, barren country July 2 required fourteen miles of detour. tour. Though the cavalry was fifteen miles from Fort Lincoln, the clear atmosphere made it look like the fort was only three or four miles away.

As the column neared the foot of Wolf Butte it was peered at by a village of prairie dogs who curiously surveyed the soldiers, then barked, and disappeared underground.

49. The alarm was sounded because a few antelope had strayed into the outer perimeter of the camp and had failed to halt on the order of the picket, who had probably mistaken the antelope for Indians.

Many such false alarms were sounded. Ewert recalled one occasion when word was passed that the camp was being attacked by 30,000 Indians. The "Indians" turned out to be bunches of grass that the excited and imaginative pickets had believed to be crawling figures.

Good grazing, a good supply of water—a plentiful supply of wood.

Arrived at Camp No. 8.[50] Marched 18 3/4 miles.

July 9

The calls were sounded at the usual time. The command moved at 5 o'clock.

The road was very good, with the exception of one bad crossing which was reached 6:45 A.M. The country all around is rich with fine grass.

In my opinion this is far better than the Yellowstone country for grazing, but so far not so good for wood. Col. Thomas W. Custer killed five antelope—caught a young rabbit. General Custer killed one antelope. We came across several high peaks (one in particular) from the crests of which you can behold the country for many miles around.

I pity some of our horses that have to carry such heavy burdens. I know of many men in the command weighing nearly two hundred pounds and add to this the weight of saddle equipments, arms, accoutrements, etc, etc. I think the poor horses have a pretty heavy load.

For instance, the Acting Assistant Adjutant General of the Expedition to my knowledge weighed 190 lbs on the Commissary scales at Fort Lincoln a few days prior to our departure, and judging from appearances I believe he has not decreased any—a pretty good load for a dumb brute.

Marched 18 42/100 miles, arrived at Camp No. 9 on Grand River. This river is a beautiful stream of running water; A gravel bottom.

---

50. Curtis reported to the *Chicago Inter-Ocean* that the Sioux guide called Goose had led them to the site where they camped on July 8. The campsite was a grassy plain at the foot of a rocky bluff covered with trees; at the base of the bluff ran a stream of clear water.

A breathtaking sunset greeted the soldiers as the intense daytime heat was subdued by a cool, fresh breeze; the band played familiar airs. This camp was a welcome change from the prairie land they had crossed for the past week, and was one of the few shady spots encountered during the week. The Indians called this spot *Pa-ha-che-cho-cha*, or Hidden Wood, because it was so surrounded by hills that it could not be seen from two miles away. *Chicago Inter-Ocean*, July 29, 1874.

Goose, an Indian Scout, informed the Commdg. Officer no timber would be seen for many miles, and that wood would have to be carried in the wagons for purposes of fuel. The Company Commanders were informed accordingly. Lt. McIntosh kicked by a horse.

July 10

The command moved at the usual hour. Crossed a branch of the Grand River 5:45 A.M., at 7:30 A.M. crossed the south side of Grand River. Recrossed same at noon to the N side.

The country travelled over is not fit for agricultural purposes. Too much gravel and stone mixed with the soil. Some portions of the table land are very rich.

The Band played several merry tunes on a high hill while the command moved up the bottom.[51] We were delayed some time owing to a bad crossing—The bottom of this river is full of alkali.

A bridge was made of wagon tongues and coupling poles which rendered a crossing practicable.

Lignite of good quality was discovered a little to our left about 18 miles from our last camp. Specimens were brought in and used at the Officer's mess. I am informed it is well adapted for fuel but not for smelting purposes.

One of the Badgers died today by being smothered in the wagon. Marched 23 65/100 miles. Arrived at Camp No. 10. For the second time we camped on Grand River. The grazing of middling quality.

July 11

The command moved at the usual hour. Crossed to the S side of Grand River. Travelled due west. Noticed too much shooting at game within the lines; if any shot were fired as a signal of danger I fear very little attention would be paid to it under existing circumstances.

---

51. The Seventh Cavalry's favorite tune was "Garry Owen"; others enjoyed by the men were "Blue Danube" and "The Mocking Bird."

The badger and rabbit died which were in possession of General C. I believe they died from neglect. Goose, an Indian Scout, and I might say guide (for this Indian has traversed this country before), informed the Commanding Officer that on our journey today we should see a cave where Indians at one time were wont to congregate for the purpose of holding intercourse with the Great Spirit.

Arrived at Camp No. 11, marched 19 3/4 miles, grazing indifferent, plenty of wood and water. A spring of cold water was found near the summit of the bluffs.

Found the cave in the rocks just above camp. The General was the first to enter it. Named it Ludlow's cave in honor of the Engineer Officer of the Expedition. I suppose the Gen'l is the first white explorer that entered it. In this cave was found many Indian equipments. Around the walls were rude carvings and inscriptions of a curious character showing different routes of travel, the range of buffalo, and the direction to the game country, and other cuts only known to Indians themselves.[52]

Some of the officers and scientific men entered the cave and went inside about 400 feet. Several of our officers scratched their names and rank on the stone wall at the entrance, so that the redskins may find the names of some who left civilization to pay them a visit and explore an unknown country.

---

52. Ewert was not very impressed with Ludlow's Cave. To Ewert it "was nothing but a rent in a cliff," and he described it as being fifteen feet wide, forty-five feet deep, and eight feet high. Some of the Sioux scouts informed Ewert that the cave had been inhabited by a white man, whose long hair and beard had been snow white. According to the Sioux, warriors had fired at him many times, often at short range, without effect. Carroll and Frost, *Ewert's Diary*.

Donaldson described the cave as being eight or ten feet in height and width and several hundred yards deep.

Ludlow, after whom the cave was named, reported the cave as being two or three hundred feet in depth with an entrance fifteen by twenty feet. Ludlow, *Reconnaissance*, p. 10.

In a letter to his wife mailed July 15, Custer indicated that the cave was four hundred feet long, and that he could not account for the Indian drawings of ships. Marguerite Merington, *The Custer Story* (New York: Devin-Adair Co., 1950), p. 273.

It was a day of belittlement for Ewert. He was tired—they had travelled twenty miles. He and his fellow troopers would have welcomed an Indian engagement just to break "the dull monotony of the daily marches." In this critical mood he wrote: "Every brook or creek, be it ever so small or insignificant, is christened a river; every mudpuddle is dubbed a creek." Carroll and Frost, *Ewert's Diary*, p. 17.

This cave put me in mind of one I saw resembling it much in Derbyshire, England, and I began to think of brighter and better days.

A skull of a white man was found near the cave. Several citizens accompanying the Expedition have spoken to me freely regarding this country. They give it as their candid opinion that should the Black Hills fail to open a country worthy of development, that there is nothing here to invite emigration and that it would be a sin and shame to encourage the poor emigrant to come hither.

July 12

Command moved as usual. Travelled over a different country—over high bluffs and rocky hills.

Several prominent points of observation, "Slim Butte," a range of hills to our right called the "Cow that Killed the Man." A high ridge in front called the "pine hills."

These hills at a distance remind me of the Welch slopes in appearance and beauty. We are travelling in a bottom full of wide and deep gullies, sage brush all over. Marched 11 miles; although we marched this distance we are not more than 5 miles in a straight line from our last camp. Arrived at Camp No. 12, wood and water. Two springs cold water—Grazing very poor indeed. Camped on high ground.[53]

July 13

A fine day. Three bad crossings. Travelled over a rough country. Indians reported on our left. Several holes were found con-

---

53. Custer always took the lead, followed by his guides and the Indian scouts under the command of Lieutenant George Wallace. Near Wallace rode a man who carried Custer's designating flag, a red and blue swallow-tailed guidon. Immediately behind them rode an escort of one company of cavalry, and following was the private ambulance that carried Custer's "collection of curiosities" that was driven by Antelope Fred.

Antelope Fred Snow had served on the frontier as a wagonmaster, foragemaster, packer, and scout, but driving Custer's private ambulance must have been one of his most difficult assignments. Custer, ardent sportsman that he was, "would chase an antelope, elk or deer over ground almost impossible for a horse," yet he would expect Snow, with his team-drawn ambulance, to be near him at all times. Frederick S. Snow, "Black Hills Expedition," 1874, manuscript package number 31, in Elizabeth B. Custer collection.

taining water but full of alkali. Many of our men suffering with dysentery caused by drinking too much alkali water. Marched 15 miles—Arrived at Camp No. 13. Grazing middling; wood and water.

General Custer obtained two young rabbits.

July 14

Travelled over a very hilly country. If the grazing had continued of poor quality I believe the mules would soon play out. The amount of forage issued to the public animals is very small. Three bad crossings. At our first halt my attention was called to dense volumes of smoke ascending from the prairie on the right of our march. This is a signal of alarm given by Indians to congregate.

At noon to day we reached a beautiful stream of water. I do not know the name, but believe it is one of the many tributaries of the "Little Missouri."

Saw remnant of an Indian wigwam—the leaves were green and could not be more than two or three days old.

Descended into a beautiful valley; commanding view of the country for many miles. Marched 13 9/10 miles, arrived at Camp No. 14. Rich grazing, good water, and an abundant supply of wood.

The Commdg. Officer give this valley a very suitable name—viz "Prospect Valley."[54]

To our right appears the "Little Missouri River" and a very heavy growth of timber is visible in that direction.

Just as the sun was setting in all his resplendent glory, large volumes of smoke were seen ascending up to the heavens—subsequently as darkness covered the earth, the sky became so red as to make it look like one great conflagration of the elements. Should the red forces wish to favor us with a little demonstra-

---

54. Custer named the area "Prospect Valley" because his two prospectors, Horatio Nelson Ross and William McKay, made their first attempts to pan gold in the creek that ran through this valley.

tion of hostilities, now is their time whilst we are in the open prairie—where we could give them a taste of lead.

A strong force of pickets was thrown out tonight.

July 15

Laid over at Camp No. 14 to give the animals rest, and allow the men an opportunity to wash their clothes.[55] The Indian Scouts were sent out in all directions. Indians reported in the vicinity of camp watching our movements. A beautiful day. The men and animals seem to enjoy the rest given them, especially the infantrymen for they were tired of marching on foot and were heard to complain of sore feet and prickly heat. Nearly 3,900 feet above the level.

It affords great pleasure to observe the great care which some of our soldiers give to their horses. A good cavalryman takes great pride in his horse, ever attentive and watchful to the interests of the latter. A looker-on can see at a glance how fond the dumb brute is of his rider. Our stock is in excellent condition and look better than when we started from Fort Lincoln.

Two Indian scouts left in the night for Fort Lincoln with the mail.[56]

The Commanding Officer sent the following dispatch to Department Headquarters.

---

55. Half of the command (five hundred men) laundered clothing in the creek. When they had finished several hours of rubbing shirts, socks, and drawers, they were as dirty as—if not dirtier than—they were when they began.

56. In Custer's letter to Libbie written and carried that night (July 15, 1874) from Prospect Valley, he indicated that the letter was being carried by two of his Arikara (Ree) scouts, Bull Bear and Skunk's Head. Apparently in a jubilant mood he wrote: "I am more convinced than ever of the influence a commanding officer exercises for good or ill. There was not a single card party, not a single drunken officer, since we left Ft. Lincoln. But I know that did I play cards and invite officers to join there would be playing every night." Marguerite Merington, *The Custer Story*, pp. 272–74. But Custer's names for the scouts may not have been accurate: Donaldson said the scouts were named Skunk's Head and Bull Neck. A. B. Donaldson, "The Black Hills Expedition," *South Dakota Historical Collections* 7(1914):554.

Headq'rs Black Hills Expedition
Prospect Valley, Dakota
July 15th, 1874

Longitude   103°46'
Latitude   45°29'

Assistant Adjutant General
    Department of Dakota
    Saint Paul, Minn.

Sir:

This expedition reached this point yesterday having marched since leaving Fort Lincoln two hundred and twenty-seven and a half miles. We are now one hundred and seventy miles in a direct line from Lincoln and within five miles of the "Little Missouri River" and within about twelve miles of the Montana boundary, our bearing from Fort Lincoln being south sixty-two degrees west. After the second day from Lincoln we marched over a beautiful country, the grazing was excellent and abundant, wood sufficient for our wants and water in great abundance every ten miles. When we struck the tributaries of Grand River we entered a less desirable portion of the country. Nearly all the streams flowing into Grand River being more or less impregnated with alkali rendering the crossings difficult. We found a plentiful supply of grass, wood and water however, even along this portion of our route.

Upon leaving the headwaters of Grand River we ascended the plateau separating the water shed of the "Little Missouri" from that running into the Missouri and found a country of surpassing beauty and richness of soil. The pasturage could not be finer, timber is abundant and water both good and plentiful. As an evidence of the character of the country, we have marched since leaving Fort Lincoln on an average of over seventeen miles per day, one day marching thirty-two miles; yet our mules and beef cattle have constantly improved in condition; the beef cattle depending entirely upon the excellent grazing we have marched over.

The health of my command is something remarkable, not a single man being on the sick report. Everyone seems not only in good health, but in excellent spirits. Between the forks of Grand River we discovered a cave to which the Indians attach great importance. The cave extends about four hundred feet under ground, beyond which point it was not practicable to explore it. Its walls and roof are covered with rude carvings and drawings cut into the solid rock, apparently the

34

work of Indians although probably by a different tribe than either of those now roaming in the region.

Near the cave was found a white man's skull apparently perforated by a bullet; it had been exposed to the atmosphere for several years. As no white men, except those belonging to this expedition are known to have passed anywhere near this locality, the discovery of this skull was regarded with unusual interest. The cave was found to contain numerous articles of Indian equipment, which had been thrown into the cave by the Indians as offerings to the "Great Spirit." I have named the cave "Ludlows Cave" in honor of the Engineer officer of the expedition.

Our march thus far has been made without molestation upon the part of the Indians. We discovered no sign indicating the recent presence of Indians until day before yesterday when Captain McDougall 7th Cavalry, who was on the flank, discovered a small party of about twenty Indians watching our movements; the Indians scampered off as soon as discovered. Yesterday the same or a similar sized party made its appearance along our line of march, and soon after several signals of smoke were sent up which our Indian guides interpret as carrying information to the main body of our presence and movements.

As I sent pacific messages to all the tribes infesting this region before the expedition moved and expressed a desire to maintain friendly relations with them, the signals observed by us may have simply been made to enable the villages to avoid us. Our Indian guides think differently however and believe the Indians mean war; should this be true, they will be the party to fire the first shot.

Indians have been seen near camp today. Mr. Grinnell of Yale College, one of the Geologists accompanying the expedition, discovered on yesterday an important fossil; it was a bone about four feet long and twelve inches in diameter and had evidently belonged to an animal larger than an elephant.

Beds of lignite of good quality have been observed at various points along our route by Professor Winchell, one of the geologists of the Expedition. I do not know whether I will be able to communicate with you again before the return of the expedition or not.

(signed)   G. A. Custer
Brevet Major General U. S. A.
Commdg. Expedition.

*

Special Orders

No. 29

I. Hereafter the commanding officers of the right and left Battalions of cavalry will detail daily one company from their respective commands to be employed as advanced guards. The commanding officers of the companies detailed for this duty will report in person to these Headquarters for special instructions immediately after Boots and Saddles has been sounded. In case hostilities occur with Indians these companies will be considered as still under the command of their respective battalion Commanders.

II. The attention of Battalion and company commanders of cavalry is called to existing orders requiring cavalry to march opposite the centre of the train. It has been observed upon several occasions recently that the cavalry has continued to advance after passing the train, thereby leaving the latter greatly exposed to attack. Now that it is known that Indians are prowling in the vicinity of our lines of march, Commanding Officers of cavalry battalions will so regulate their march that at least one company of each of their respective commands, not including the rear guard, marches in rear of the centre of the train.

III. Should this command become engaged with hostile Indians, the rear guard and pioneer company will act under the orders of their respective Battalion Commanders.[57]

By order of Brevet Major General Custer.

Signed   James Calhoun
          1st Lieut., 7th Cavalry
          A. A. A. G.

*

---

57. Although Custer was still leading, he was now sending his Indian scouts ahead, since they knew where in the country the troops could find wood, water, and game. Based on his scouts' reports, Custer made the final determination as to the route best suited for a wagon train.

Fred Powers of the *St. Paul Press* remarked in a report published on July 15 that the marches had varied since the column had left Fort Lincoln: the distance covered was between fifteen and thirty miles each day and was determined by the availability of wood and water. And, he said, most of the water was alkali.

In his dispatch written from Prospect Valley to the *St. Paul Pioneer* that day, Donaldson had drawn the conclusion that "guides know the country as to wood, water, and game, but their judgment as to practicable wagon routes cannot be relied upon." He had experienced some of their errors of judgment with the resultant detours, which made him feel "traveling through such country as this, with the thermometer at 100 in the shade, takes the enthusiasm all out of a neophyte."

July 16

The Command moved at 4:50 A.M.—travelled in the valley of the "Little Missouri." High hills in the distance. Short pine ridge to our right which I am informed leads to the Powder River Country—Charles Reynolds, one of the guides, saw quite a number of Indians on the right of our march.[58]

After the command had moved about 21 miles up the valley of the Little Missouri orders were given to fill the kegs with water, and load the wagons with wood. Ascended the bluffs to our left. I would here remark I noticed a heavy growth of timber all along our route up the valley, and in some portions of the Little Missouri there is abundance of everything capable of sustaining a dense population.[59] Arrived at Camp No. 15 at sundown.

But Custer was no neophyte. His effervescent spirit and abundant energy were augmented rather than diminished by this life. With all that came under his supervision, he still found time to bedevil his brother Boston. But the general was not alone: others had also taken it upon themselves to practice jokes on the good-natured Bos (as Boston was affectionately called). Bos put rocks in a wash basin to soak each night because his brother Tom assured him they were sponge stones and would soften when soaked. After a few unsuccessful nights, Bos wised up.

Relating another frolic, Custer wrote to Libbie, (Elizabeth B. Custer, *Boots and Saddles*, p. 300) about Bos riding a mule that displayed endurance but no aptitude for speed. While Bos rode beside Custer one day, the land ahead was so undulating that one could see far ahead from the top of each divide, but one could not see down into the gullies. Custer told Bos that he needed to go forward. Galloping his horse Vic slowly over the divide, Custer put spurs to him when they were out of Bos's sight, galloping the horse rapidly over the intervening low ground. When he came into Bos's sight again, Custer was moving slowly up the next divide, calling for Bos to hurry. Bos would shout at his mule and wave his arms and legs in an attempt to hurry him. As he neared the next divide, Custer would again disappear over it and again give Vic the rein until Bos reappeared. This went on for some time, and Bos couldn't understand why the distance between them grew so rapidly when both seemed to travel at the same gait. Finally Bos discovered the joke.

58. In his recollections, Antelope Fred Snow noted that large numbers of Indians were seen that day on all sides, and that Bear Butte could be faintly seen to the southeast. He was also the only one to report that a Dakota zephyr (a west wind) struck the camp that night, blowing down tents and causing the horses to stampede. The wind, he said, was accompanied by a heavy rain. Snow, "Black Hills Expedition."

But apparently Snow was inaccurate as to the date of the storm. Ludlow reported a severe windstorm for the following night, July 17.

59. The Little Missouri River was a rapidly moving stream eighteen inches deep and thirty to forty feet wide. The banks averaged forty feet in height even though the valley was several miles wide.

Donaldson had all he wanted of "this valley of disappointment." The thirty-one miles of travel that day took seventeen hours of heat and dust—enough to dry up any man's interest.

Marched 30 1/5 miles. Camped on an elevated portion of the country. No wood and only a few holes of alkali water. Grazing poor.

General Custer obtained two rattlesnakes.

On our march today we saw a high point resembling a lighthouse; named it "Light House Point." Another beautiful hill presented itself to our view. Looking at the distance you would naturally think there were several fine mansions erected. One of these presented an imposing sight and in my opinion resembled the Crystal Palace, London, but the Engineer Officer said it looked more like the Capitol, and it was named "Capitol Butte."

Crossed over a trail supposed to be Gen'l Connor's Expedition to the Powder River country.

July 17

The command moved at 5 o'clock. Two more rattlesnakes added to the family. Saw an Indian trail.[60]

In full view of the Black Hills.

Two extensive fires from the direction of the Black Hills—at midnight the very heavens seemed on fire. Marched 18 miles. Arrived at Camp No. 16. No wood, very little water.[61]

July 18

Reveille 1/2 an hour later than usual. Descended into a strip of "Bad Lands" leading to the "Big Cheyenne" valley. This strip has the appearance of a barren waste.

---

60. Bloody Knife reported that a large party of Indians had crossed in front of them dragging travois poles. This signified an Indian village on the move. Snow, "Black Hills Expedition."

61. Donaldson felt no greater joy on July 17 than he had on the preceding day. As the expedition botanist, there was little along the route to excite him. Other than greaseweed, "nothingness of vegetation" greeted him. As he said in his July 25 report to the *Pioneer*: "The better parts of this miserable region are settled by prairie dogs and rattlesnakes. The command and a few estrayed grasshoppers are the only visitors."

6:20, bad crossing over a creek. The water of this creek is as bitter as gall—very miry. A portion of the command anticipate a little Indian warfare today, and the men are exceedingly anxious to give the Indians a free taste of lead whilst we are in an open country. The prevailing impression is that the Indians will not attack us until we get in the interior of the Black Hills, when they will have a decided advantage over us. Bushwhacking with unseen enemies is a game of warfare not to be desired. From the general appearance of the country in our front, it is believed if they strike a blow at us from places of ambush and the surrounding fortifications, that they will have too much their own way, and may probably get the best of us.

10 A.M. arrived at a beautiful stream of pure water. Bad crossing command delayed for nearly two hours.

2 P.M. Encountered another bad crossing. The country travelled over was very rough and caused the wagon train to be strung out for more than two miles thereby leaving portions thereof unprotected. But we soon reached a more desirable country, inviting and beautiful. Before us were fine groves of heavy timber. Large pine and abundant growth of oak timber. The first oak I have seen for many a day. Descended into the valley of the "Big Cheyenne." Oh! this is indeed a delightful place. Arrived at Camp No. 17, marched 17 1/2 miles. Excellent grazing. A branch of the North fork of the "Big Cheyenne" running through our camp. Abundant quantity of wood. From the appearance of the country I believe we will have no more trouble regarding the fuel matter.

Orders were given to have all the water kegs filled. Captain Reynolds passed through this country 15 years ago. Saw his trail running through our camp.[62] I presume there was a camp in this vicinity when Capt. Reynolds passed by this way.

---

62. Ludlow drew attention to two unbroken rows of sunflowers, wagon wheels apart, as far as one could see in either direction. The sod had been broken by the wheels of the former expedition under the command of Reynolds during the time the sunflowers were in bloom. The seeds had fallen into the wagon ruts. William R. Wood, "Reminiscence," manuscript, 1927, Minnesota Historical Society.

July 19

Owing to the wet weather the Command did not move today. The supply train was moved across the river this afternoon, the Infantry Battalion following as guard.

July 20

The command moved at 5 o'clock. Had to travel over a very hilly country. Passed through a magnificent country. The finest quality of grass I ever saw. Large forests of pine and oak timber. The valleys are beautiful indeed and full of picturesque scenery. This is a better country than I expected to find. What endless enjoyment for the finite mind to contemplate the wonderful works of nature. Here nature spreads herself open in a conspicuous manner.

As I gaze upon this particular spot, I think that it is a great pity that this rich country should remain in a wild state, uncultivated and uninhabited by civilized men. Here the wheel of industry could move to advantage. The propelling power of life in the shape of human labor is only wanting to make this a region of prosperity.

True happiness is obtained by contentment, constant exercise of the body, the brain in full motion, with a mellifluous desire to ameliorate the condition of mankind. Man is the promoter of earthly happiness. He is the divine instrument, pre-ordained from primitive existence to diffuse this beneficence upon the earth. Man is the noblest work of God. In this wild region man will ultimately be seen in the full enjoyment of true pleasure, in the possession of happiness obtained by honest labor. For the hives of industry will take the place of dirty wigwams. Civilization will ere long reign supreme and throw heathen barbarism into oblivion. Seminaries of learning will raise their proud cupolas far above the canopy of Indian lodges, and Christian temples will elevate their lofty spires upward towards the azure sky while places of heathen mythology will sink to rise no more. This will be a period of true happiness.

Having received permission from the Commanding Officer to ride near the Engineer party at the head of the train I frequently have opportunity to converse with some who are thoroughly acquainted with the Great West. For information I asked several citizens accompanying the Expedition their opinion regarding the country travelled over today, and they told me freely that up to yesterday they had formed a very unfavorable impression concerning this region, but this morning their unfavorable opinions vanished like the "morning cloud and early dew," and they were astonished to behold such a sudden change. That it eclipsed anything they ever saw before, and that the valleys passed through could not be surpassed for agricultural purposes and natural beauty.

Marched 19 91/100 miles—arrived at Camp No. 18. Excellent pasturage, a spring of cold water. Not much water for the public animals. I am informed that early this A.M. we arrived at the foot of the Black Hills.[63]

July 21

A beautiful morning. At 10 o'clock A.M. came to a beautiful creek, from which good cold water was obtained for man and beast.

Private Hoener, Company B, 7th Cavalry, accidentally shot himself in the leg.

From reliable source—viz—from persons whom I know to be well posted regarding this country I am informed that Indian ponies wintered in the Black Hills all come out fat in the spring, and that this range is well adapted for stock raising.

This is also one of the most desirable spots in the west for sheep raising.[64] I will here give my reasons for making this statement. The winters here are not so severe. Protected from the inclemency of the weather by the high hills the valleys are rendered temperate and suitable for the breeding of sheep. There is also an abundant quantity of nutritious food to be found in the win-

---

63. Ludlow confirms arrival at this geographical location in his report.

64. It has been observed that by autumn a lamb running in the forests of the Black Hills will frequently weigh ten pounds more than one that has been grazing on the range all summer. R. E. Driscoll, *Seventy Years of Banking in the Black Hills* (Rapid City, S.D.: Gate City Guide Publishers, 1948), p. 56.

ter season between the many and immense mountains affording as much, if not more nourishment than any other part of the same latitude. The excellent herbage, and nutritious grass are of perennial growth, capable of giving satisfaction to the beasts of pasture. Four bad crossings.

Marched 14 3/10 miles—arrived at Camp No. 19, a delightful spring of cold water—sufficient for man and beast. Abundant quantity of wood. Private John Cunningham, Company H, 7th Cavalry, who has been sick for a few days past, died at 11 o'clock tonight.[65]

The General obtained a large piece of petrified wood.

A portion of the ground passed over was of a red clayey soil, and I am informed it is well adapted for making brick.

---

65. Cunningham had been sick for some time with chronic diarrhea, dying finally from complications of concomitant acute pleurisy. Two others died from digestive disorders before the expedition reached Fort Lincoln. Sergeant Windolph said that digestive disorders and diarrhea were so common that the troopers would have to hurriedly dismount and dicharge their bowels. On rainy days the soldiers were even more uncomfortable because of the high wet grass. R. G. Cartwright to Lawrence A. Frost, February 28, 1974, Lawrence A. Frost collection.

Ewert recalled in his diary that Cunningham became ill with acute dysentery about July 13. When Cunningham went on sick call, the contract doctor refused to relieve him from duty. His illness increased in severity; he petitioned the doctor four days later, and again he was refused relief from duty. The following day, Cunningham, "through weakness and loss of blood, fainted and fell off his horse." Bitterly, Ewert relates how Colonel Benteen ordered Sergeant Connelley to take the sick man to an ambulance, where Ewert saw Cunningham lying there in a coma, exposed to the raw rays of the sun.

"Butcher" Allen, as Ewert and the men afterward called the doctor in charge (Acting Assistant Surgeon S. J. Allen), was then, and Ewert says, was most of the time, drunk. Unable to obtain service from Allen, Ewert appealed to Calhoun, who "took the matter to heart, went immediately, and with great effort awoke Dr. Williams." Chief Medical Officer J. W. Williams, also drunk, staggered to the ambulance, looked at the dying man for a moment, then staggered back to his tent, where he fell on his bed and slept.

Ewert, now quite concerned, sent word to the men of his company that Cunningham was dying. In a matter of minutes he was surrounded by a dozen men who debated whether to summon Custer. Donaldson happened by and asked the cause of the gathering; when he heard the details, he went directly to Custer. Custer sent for Williams. Upon seeing the sorry state the intoxicated Williams was in, Custer dismissed him and sent for Allen. Allen, also still intoxicated, insisted that Cunningham was not dying. He prescribed a few opium pills for Cunningham and then left the scene. Cunningham died that night at 11:25. Thereafter the men never referred to Allen and Williams as doctors, but rather as "Butcher" Allen or "Drunken" Williams. Carroll and Frost, *Ewert's Diary*, pp. 32–36.

Passing through Castle Valley

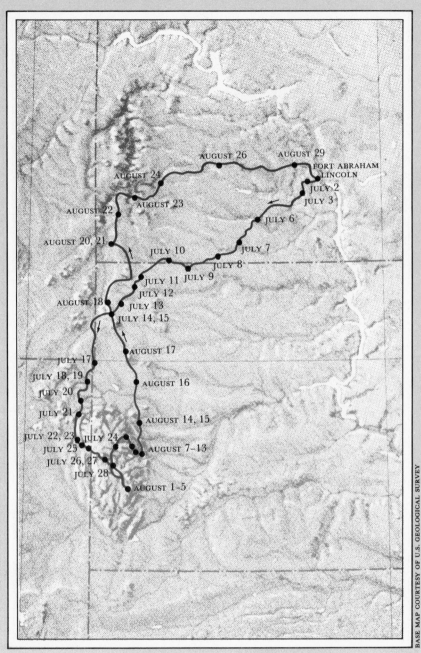

AUGUST 26   AUGUST 29

AUGUST 24   FORT ABRAHAM
                                       LINCOLN

AUGUST 23   JULY 2
AUGUST 22   JULY 3

                          JULY 6
AUGUST 20, 21

          JULY 10   JULY 7

               JULY 8

JULY 11 JULY 9
         JULY 12
AUGUST 18 JULY 13
          JULY 14, 15

               AUGUST 17

JULY 17
JULY 18, 19   AUGUST 16
JULY 20
JULY 21   AUGUST 14, 15
JULY 22, 23 JULY 24
JULY 25   AUGUST 7–13
JULY 26, 27
JULY 28
          AUGUST 1–5

BASE MAP COURTESY OF U.S. GEOLOGICAL SURVEY

Entire Route of the 1874 Black Hills Expedition

44

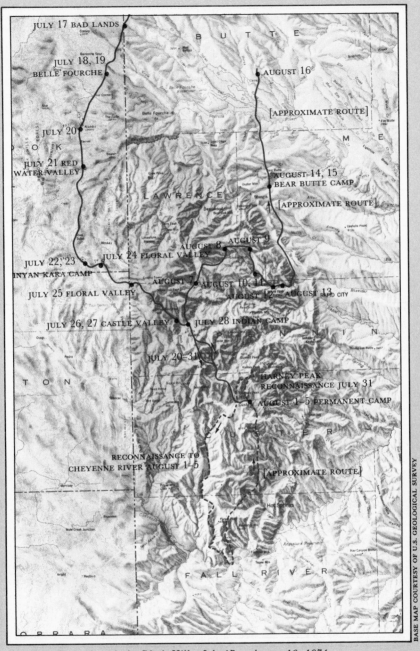

JULY 17 BAD LANDS

JULY 18, 19
BELLE FOURCHE

AUGUST 16

[APPROXIMATE ROUTE]

JULY 20

JULY 21 RED
WATER VALLEY

AUGUST 14, 15
BEAR BUTTE CAMP

[APPROXIMATE ROUTE]

AUGUST 8   AUGUST 9
AUGUST 7   FLORAL VALLEY
JULY 24 FLORAL VALLEY

JULY 22, 23
INYAN KARA CAMP

JULY 25 FLORAL VALLEY

AUGUST 10, 11
AUGUST 12   AUGUST 13
RAPID CITY

JULY 26, 27 CASTLE VALLEY   JULY 28 INDIAN CAMP

JULY 20-31

HARNEY PEAK
RECONNAISSANCE JULY 31
AUGUST 1-5 PERMANENT CAMP

RECONNAISSANCE TO
CHEYENNE RIVER AUGUST 1-5

[APPROXIMATE ROUTE]

BASE MAP COURTESY OF U.S. GEOLOGICAL SURVEY

Expedition Route through the Black Hills, July 17 to August 16, 1874

45

Posing on the Rock
James Calhoun is on the right

First Grizzly
George A. Custer
August 7, 1874

Officers
Top, Frederick T. Grant; center left, George
A. Custer; lower right, Frederick W. Benteen

Resting
Left to right: William Ludlow, George Yates,
Thomas W. Custer

Ready to March

Bivouac on the Prairie

Summary table of daily instrumental observations, with deduced altitudes, the latitude and longitude of each camp, distances traveled, &c.

Date	Location	Start	Arrive	Thermometer Max.	Min.	No.	Total.	Mean.	Barometer Evening.	Morning.	Elevation.	Latitude.	Longitude.	Day's march.	Total distance.	Heights of peaks above sea-level, in feet.
1874				°	°			°			Feet.	° ′ ″	° ′ ″	Miles.	Miles.	
July 2	Back Creek	8.00 a.m.	8.45 p.m.	94	70	3	260	86.6	27.66	27.60	2,169	46 40 50	101 03 08	15.1	15.1	
3	Dog's Teeth Creek	8.00 a.m.	3.00 p.m.	98½	83	3	272	90.6	27.85		1,930	46 35 25	101 06 43	14.1	29.2	
4	Creek "where bear winters"	4.30 a.m.	11.30 a.m.	78	64	5	434	88.2	27.74	27.68	2,090			14.7	43.9	
5	Cannon Ball River	4.45 a.m.	1.00 p.m.	78	59	5	342	68.4	27.56	27.56	2,251	46 19 52	101 47 43	16.9	60.8	
6	Cedar Creek	4.30 a.m.	10.00 a.m.	94	60	5	392	77.1	27.36		2,439	46 03 39	102 06 07	12.9	73.7	
7	Hidden Wood Creek	7.00 a.m.	4.30 p.m.	84	64	4	308.5	76.8	27.34	27.32	2,345	45 54 58	102 45 43	30.4	104.1	
8	Grand River	4.45 a.m.	2.30 p.m.	100	46	4	384	67.5	27.45	27.57	2,608	45 58 00	103 01 42	10.0	123.1	
9	do	4.50 a.m.	4.00 p.m.	83	45	6	470	79.3	27.20	27.15	2,439	45 49 10	103 36 46	20.0	143.1	
10	Cave	5.45 a.m.	1.00 p.m.	87	62	5	476	79.3	26.43	26.63	3,189	45 43 43	103 29 10	24.0	167.1	
11	Sage Brush Camp	5.00 a.m.	1.00 p.m.	90	62	5	405	81.0	26.61	26.61	3,189	45 35 45	103 38 55	19.7	186.8	
12	Prospect Valley	4.45 a.m.	2.00 p.m.	87	56	5	335.5	67.3	26.58	26.57	3,271	45 35 50	103 38 10	13.5	213.3	
13	Border Camp	4.45 a.m.	2.20 p.m.	82	56	5	357.5	71.3	26.38	26.36	3,488	45 28 56	103 47 25	13.0	226.3	
14, 15	Bad Lands	4.45 a.m.	4.15 p.m.	89	53	4	328	82.0	26.54		3,054			30.7	256.8	
16, 17	Belle Fourche	5.00 a.m.	4.30 p.m.	78	63	37	2,644.6	71.5	26.84	26.84	3,734	44 46 10	104 02 20	17.5	292.0	
18, 19	Red Water Valley	4.45 a.m.	5.00 p.m.	91	51	36	1,411	73.6	26.16		3,926	44 38 35	104 15 57	18.3	310.3	
20	Inyan Kara Camp	4.45 a.m.	4.30 p.m.	86	73	11	1,333.3	77.3	25.85	25.75	4,565	44 13 00	104 15 32	14.3	324.6	Inyan Kara, 6,500.
22, 23	Floral Valley	4.45 a.m.	5.00 p.m.	86	61	11	842.7	76.6	24.69	24.69	6,196	44 12 40	104 11 30	11.5	346.8	
24	do	4.45 a.m.	3.15 p.m.	86	60	9	80	86.0	24.84	24.63	6,345	44 03 34	104 03 34	11.0	357.8	
26, 27	Castle Valley	4.45 a.m.	2.00 p.m.	66	40	9	591.2	70.7	23.89	23.82	6,925	44 01 43	104 03 54	12.0	369.3	
28, 29	Indian Camp	4.45 a.m.	3.00 p.m.	93	46	9	646	71.8	24.51	24.54	5,903	44 04 48	104 48 57	14.0	383.3	
30, 31 Aug. 1–5	Permanent Camp	7.00 a.m.	1.00 p.m.	82	46	12	895	74.6	24.50	24.50	5,664	43 46 10	103 33 02	10.5	418.7	Harney's Peak, 9,700.
6		4.45 a.m.	7.30 p.m.	71	65	4	308	69.8	24.35	24.53	5,768			13.3	432.2	
7		4.55 a.m.	5.30 p.m.	89	63	3	152	76.0	24.39	24.23	5,768	44 08 53	103 43 50	16.2	448.4	
8		4.15 a.m.							24.34	24.33	5,484	44 15 10	103 38 08	14.7	461.6	
9		4.45 a.m.							24.49	24.69	5,633			7.5	476.3	
10, 11		4.45 a.m.	7.00 p.m.	72	49	6	416	52.2	24.96	24.94	4,963	44 03 16	103 30 16	5.7	483.8	
12, 13		12.00 m.	2.00 p.m.	57	68	4	201	58.2	25.84	25.64	4,364	44 07 46	103 23 48	13.3	497.0	
14, 15	Bear Butte Camp	4.45 a.m.	7.00 p.m.	90	66	8	583	77.7	25.36	25.30	4,318	44 07 35	103 20 49	4.0	501.7	Bear Butte, 4,800.
16		4.45 a.m.	7.00 p.m.	88	54	10	1,449	72.3	26.09	25.60	3,889	44 11 33	103 37 45	26.0	527.7	
17	Prospect Valley	4.45 a.m.	7.00 p.m.	81	62	10	730	66.4	25.75	25.77	3,667	45 31 05	103 22 35	28.2	555.4	
18, 19		4.45 a.m.	7.15 p.m.	84	52	4	891	63.6	25.75	25.63	3,475			30.2	585.4	
20, 21	Little Missouri River	4.45 a.m.		74	66	28	1,334	69.7	26.00	26.05	3,533	46 08 30	103 21 30	29.3	615.6	
22, 23		5.00 a.m.		83	59	15	1,088	72.5	26.30	26.39	3,296	46 27 08	103 42 54	28.5	650.9	
24	Heart River	4.45 a.m.		78	51	16	1,070	66.9	27.12	27.09	3,244	46 34 45	103 59 25	19.0	688.9	
25	Young Men's Buttes	4.45 a.m.	12.00 m.	87	33	11	751	68.3	27.15	27.00	2,719			17.7	709.3	
26		4.45 a.m.	5.00 p.m.	87	64	15	1,910	76.4	26.90	26.90	2,965	46 32 30	102 15 49	32.2	728.3	
27		4.30 a.m.		68	61	11	429	63.8	27.57	27.53	2,698			21.6	755.0	
28	Little Muddy Creek	4.45 a.m.		86	62	12	795	66.6	27.38	27.30	2,384			17.3	770.7	
29	White Fish Creek	4.45 a.m.	10.50 a.m.	83	62	13	865	66.5	27.52	27.55	1,994	46 52 00	101 16 18	32.9	802.9	
30	Fort Abraham Lincoln	4.00 a.m.		99	58	30	1,507	73.3	27.70	27.65	2,011	46 46 10	100 20 57	50.0	856.0	

RECONNAISSANCES.

		Distance	Total.
July 31	Colonel Ludlow	100	
Aug. 3 to 5	do	16	136 miles.
July 27	Lieutenant Godfrey	8	
July 31	do	20	104 miles.
Aug. 2 to 5	do	30	
7	do	6	

		Distance.	Total.
July 25	Mr. W. H. Wood	29	
July 27	do		29 }
	Sergeant Becker	13	13 } 322 miles.
July 31	Sergeant Wilson	16	16 }
	do	16	

Wagon-train traveled .... 863.3 miles.
Reconnaissances, traveled ...... 332.0 miles.

Total .... 1,195.3 miles.

Camps 47

CHIEF ENGINEER'S OFFICE, Saint Paul, Minn., April 23, 1875.

O

16 B H

Statistical table of the expedition compiled by Captain William Ludlow reproduced from his Report of a Reconnaissance of the Black Hills of Dakota Made in the Summer of 1874 (Washington, D.C.: Govt. Printing Office, 1875), p. 121.

48

July 22

The command moved at 5 o'clock. The heat is very oppressive.

Early this morning two privates of Company M, 7th Cavalry, named respectively Geo. Turner and William Roller, quarrelled about a trivial affair, which resulted in the latter shooting the former.[66]

After travelling about 18 miles we descended into an elegant valley. The most beautiful valley yet seen, full of picturesque scenery, charming and lovely—a perfect paradise. On entering this valley to our right we discovered a spring of pure water, flowing sweetly from the rocks, and as we had not seen any water since we started from camp this morning, this spring of transparent fluid was greatly invigorating. In our march many steep ascents were made but on the whole the roads were good.

Indian trails visible in all directions. Travelled in the direction of a high mountain and camped in rear of it. Arrived at Camp

---

66. Both Roller and Turner had joined M Company of the Seventh Cavalry four years earlier as recruits. Prior to this they had had a disagreement that had led to a fight, which Turner had lost. Turner, being quarrelsome by nature, couldn't forget it. He egged Roller into another fight, which Roller lost. Turner, not yet satisfied, heaped insults and abuse on Roller at every opportunity. Aggravated by this persecution, Roller agreed to fight once more, thinking it would end Turner's efforts to drive him from M Company. Roller lost for the second time. Roller then told Turner this should end the matter and "that if he still persisted in his prosecution [sic] he, Roller, would make use of his revolver as his only safety." The persecutions temporarily ceased.

On the morning of July 22, Roller found his horse crosshobbled (the right forefoot was chained to the left hindfoot so the horse couldn't move without falling). When he saw the pitiful condition of his horse, Roller swore he would whip the man who did it. Roller said "that a man who would be guilty of such an act was only to be considered a dirty son-of-a-bitch."

Turner heard Roller's exclamation and came running out of his tent, demanding to know whether the threat was intended for him. Roller said that it was meant for the man who had cross-hobbled his horse. Turner insisted it was meant for him, and announced that he was going to take it that way. Turner threw his hand to his right side where he generally carried his revolver, forgetting that just that morning he had changed his revolver to his left side.

Roller, seeing Turner reach for his gun, pulled his own gun and fired one shot that entered Turner's abdomen and lodged in his spine. Turner was placed in an ambulance, where he died about 2:00 p. m. He received no sympathy from the men. Roller gave himself up immediately after the shooting and was placed under infantry guard until he arrived at Fort Lincoln, where civil authorities would try him on a charge of murder. Carroll and Frost, *Ewert's Diary*, pp. 36–40.

No. 20 on a beautiful creek with good pasturage—marched 22 1/2 miles.

Private George Turner , Co M., 7th Cavalry, breathed his last at 3:20 P.M. Just before he expired he entered into conversation with Captain T. H. French 7th Cavalry, his company commander.

The following circulars were published at 5 o'clock:

Headq'rs Black Hills Expedition
Camp No. 20, M. T.
July 22nd, 1874

Circular No. 21

The command will not move in the morning.

By order of Br't Maj. General Custer

James Calhoun
1st Lieut., 7th Cavalry
A. A. A. General.

*

Headq'rs Black Hills Expedition
Camp No. 22, M. T.
July 22nd, 1874

Circular No. 22

The funeral ceremonies of the late Privates John Cunningham, Company H, 7th Cavalry, and George Turner, Company M, 7th Cavalry, will take place this evening at 8 o'clock.

Companies will be marched to the place of interment by the first Sergeants. All members of this command are invited to attend.

By order of Brevet Major General Custer

James Calhoun
1st Lieut., 7th Cavalry
A. A. A. G.

*

The Chief Medical Officer of the Expedition held a post mortem examination upon the body of the late Private George Turner, Company M, 7th Cavalry, and found that the ball passed through the right arm direct through the liver and lodged in the back bone. At 8 o'clock the funeral cortege assembled in front of Headquarters. The Band played the dead march and the funeral procession moved to a little knoll just below the bluffs where a grave had been dug, and the last remains of these two soldiers were buried with military honors.[67]

Life is short, death is sure. These two men were young; one this morning in the full bloom of life, the other a few days ago in the full enjoyment of good health—but now are numbered with the dead—gone to that place from whence no traveller returns.

Though buried in the Indian country far away from their paternal homes, their bodies were deposited into the grave with great solemnity, and received the last rites of a Christian burial.

This should remind us of our ultimate destiny. For one thing is certain

> "Where'eer we be,
>   what'eer we do!
> We're travelling to the grave."

Man is prone to think that all are mortal but himself, forgetting the language of the poet in one of his sublime stanzas

> "And am I only born to die,
> And must I suddenly comply;
> With natures stern decree?"

July 23

Pursuant to circular No. 21 the command did not move today. Gen'l Custer with scientific party and 2 companies of cavalry (L & M) left at 6 A. M. to explore the mountain mentioned yesterday, Inyan Kara.[68]

---

67. The funeral services for Cunningham and Turner were held that evening (July 22) at 9:00 p. m., the entire cavalry regiment attending. With the soldiers forming a hollow square around the grave, the two bodies were lowered; the service was read by the light of a lantern. Three volleys were fired over the grave; taps were blown by the trumpeter. Once the grave was filled and leveled off, a fire was kept burning over it during all of the next day as a method of hiding the grave from Indians, who sometimes dug up remains and scalped them. A. B. Donaldson, *St. Paul Pioneer*, July 25, 1874.

68. Inyan Kara, according to expedition geologist Newton H. Winchell, is a corruption of the Indian word *Heéng-ya Ha-gá*. Governor K. Warren had estimated its height to be 6,600 feet when he visited that site in 1859. Ludlow, *Reconnaissance*, p. 34.

July 24

We travelled through the hills and encountered many bad roads. I never thought it possible that a wagon train could move in such a country.

Many fine elk horns of large size were obtained; several deer killed.

On our march we reached two springs of good cold water. The first one on our right about five miles from our last camp, the other on our left 10 miles and close to our present camp. A large forest of fine pine of immense growth, well adapted for building purposes.

Ate some fine strawberries.

Arrived at Camp No. 21. Marched 11 miles. Camped in a narrow valley; a beautiful running stream of water.

The prospectors accompanying the expedition were busy this evening digging for the precious metal, but failed to find it.[69]

July 25

The command moved at 4:50 A. M.—Traveled up the valley, crossed the stream ten times, built bridges of pine poles in seven

---

69. It has been stated that the two prospectors, Ross and McKay, were Custer's guests and were paid by Custer to accompany the expedition; no record or correspondence has been found to prove it. Further, no money had been budgeted to pay any scientific members of the expedition, even though Ludlow had requested (and been denied) permission to hire a geologist at $150 a month. Donaldson, the expedition botanist, doubled as a correspondent for the *St. Paul Pioneer*.

Salaries of the civilian employees were as follows:
One chief herder: $100 per month
One herder: $60 per month
One interpreter: $100 per month
Two guides: $100 per month
One trainmaster: $100 per month
Four assistant trainmasters: $45 per month
One assistant trainmaster: $50 per month
Ninety-five teamsters: $30 per month
Five teamsters (hired enroute): $30 per month
One blacksmith: $75 per month
One wheelwright: $75 per month
One saddler: $75 per month
("Returns, Black Hills Expedition," *Records of the Office of Adjutant General*, Records Group No. 94, June–September 1874.)

different places. As we ascended, the stream became wider and deeper—clear as crystal. This whole valley is full of beautiful flowers; many fine bouquets were obtained in a few minutes. I understand this particular locality has been named "Floral Valley," an appellation that is very appropriate.

Arrived at Camp No. 22. Marched 11 85/100 miles. Camped at the headspring of the stream. Our camp is in the same valley we encamped in yesterday and owing to the want of breadth it is unavoidably scattered.[70] Grazing indifferent. Genl C. obtained a crane.

July 26

The command moved at the usual hour. Came across a late Indian camp. Could see where the Indians had cut lodge poles from the small timber suited for this purpose, a trail about 24 hours old. Our march continued through the valley—arrived at a large stream of water where the pioneer company built a bridge. Wagon train delayed about one hour and a half. Saw a "beaver dam."

Four beautiful springs of cold water. These springs sweetly flowing from the mountains are very refreshing and contain the purest water man ever drank.

Many prominent places of rough-looking stone resembling so many fortresses. I also noticed some that reminded me of several old English castles.[71] I ascended the summit of several high hills for the purpose of taking a good view of the surrounding country. I could see open spaces between the timbered hills, just like valley after valley rushing into existence presenting a grand sight, pleasing to the eye.

In the distance beautiful rocks of a carmine color were visible, adjoining a large mass of stony matter having the likeness of a Casern near ramparts.

---

70. An old, much-used lodge trail, which one of the guides said was an old voyageur pack trail, ran up Floral Valley. There were evidences of many old camps: tepee poles were stacked in large heaps, and numerous stakes where hides and furs had been stretched to dry remained in the ground.

71. Because of the rock formations, Custer named this Castle Valley.

The advance party consisting of detachment of Indian scouts and Companies C and E, 7th Cavalry, under command of Genl. Custer at 10 o'clock A. M. arrived at a point nearly fourteen miles from our last camp which was chosen for our camp today and discovered signs of the immediate presence of Indians. Fires were still burning, deer meat on the ground, pony tracks not one hour old; skeletons of wigwams and lodge poles on which their tepees had been recently hung. The Commanding Officer mandated some Indian scouts to follow the trail, and scout around with a view of obtaining some further or more desirable information.

Two Indian scouts returned after a brief absence and reported the whereabouts of these Indians. Orders were given for E & C Companies to saddle up and go forward with the Commandg. Officer. Proceeding at a rapid rate to a distance of nearly three miles, they came within sight of an Indian encampment, when three scouts and one interpreter were ordered to go into the Indian camp with a flag of truce in the shape of a white towel tied on a stick. In the meantime the command in ambush surrounded the place to prevent egress or flight on the part of the Indians.

Everything passed off favorably & the Commdg. Officer and a portion of his command went into the village, and found a small hunting party of Indians and very few of the male portion at home.[72]

I am informed that they are Ogallala Sioux and belong to "Red Cloud's" band.

---

72. The Indian village apparently consisted of five lodges (Ludlow was the only one to report seven) and twenty-seven inhabitants, five of whom were warriors. The Indians had been hunting in the Black Hills for two months and had been unaware of the troops' presence.

At the discovery of the village, the Arikaras with Custer's expedition had stripped and painted for war. Bloody Knife, whose son had been killed by Sioux several days before the expedition had left Fort Lincoln, demanded for his scouts the right to kill and scalp all hostiles, since they had discovered the camp. Custer refused by reminding Bloody Knife that all the captives were his—by virtue of his position as commanding officer—and not those of the scouts. By restricting Bloody Knife and the other scouts, Custer indicated his intention of conducting a peaceful expedition.

Through the interpreter, Custer told those in the camp that the Great White Father in Washington had sent him into the Black Hills to determine what kind of country it was and whether the Sioux had a good reservation. Custer emphasized that they had come to look and to make a map, but not to fight. Carroll and Frost, *Ewert's Diary*, p. 46.

The General subsequently sat down, and had a parlance with them, amid the smoky vapors of a peace pipe.

In the evening four of these Indians came on a visit to our camp, and after staying awhile two of them left. The other two remained in our camp for the purpose of begging rations. By a premeditated plan it was arranged that while the two Indians were in our camp, the Indians left behind should strike their teepees and flee from our presence. What their motives were it is hard to tell. Probably they were afraid of the Ree scouts.

As the Commanding Officer intended laying over one day at this camp, it was his desire to have them come and see him with a view of obtaining information regarding this country. To this end he wished some of his scouts to stay with the Indians during the night, but from the actions of the two Indians who were leaving us after obtaining rations, he evidently smelt a rat and had reason to believe they intended to slight his wishes, and treat the same with contempt. They had not proceeded far when Indian scouts were sent after them telling them to wait and also at the same time informing them more explicitly the expressed wish of the Commanding Officer, but in lieu of receiving the messengers with proper respect one of the number tried to disarm a scout of his musket and showed prompt signs of being hostile, whereupon the Indian scout dismounted and fired, and it is believed that he wounded the Indian pony. But the other Indian "One Stab" was overtaken and brought back a prisoner. "One Stab" is 63 years of age and has many a wrinkle in his face, and other marks indicative of the imbecility of old age.

He is guarded by soldiers, and the Commdg. Officer has so fixed it that during his incarceration the Indian scouts will have no chance of gobbling him up. It is well known the Arickarees or Rees have a perfect hatred against the Sioux Indians, and those of this tribe accompanying the Expedition would be glad of an opportunity to scalp "One Stab" as an offset, in the way of settling old accounts for many injuries received from the Sioux nation.[73]

---

73. The uneasiness of the Sioux could be attributed to the presence of the Rees, whose intentions were obvious, decorated as they were in war paint.

An excellent stream of pure water flowing right through our camp called "Castle Creek." Arrived at Camp No. 23 in "Castle Valley"; marched 13 97/100 miles.

Very good grazing, in some portions of our camp the grass was so high that our horses could not be seen excepting a portion of their bodies.

July 27

Laid over—Companies H & F, 7th Cavalry, divided into platoons, went out scouting accompanied by the Engineers and scientific party. A detachment found an Indian saddle & equipments, also a quantity of rations which were issued to one of the Indians mentioned yesterday, so there is no doubt but our Indian scout wounded the pony and he had to abandon these articles to lighten the weight, for the purpose of getting out of the way.

The soldiers are exceedingly pleased with the expedition, and think it a pleasure excursion.

Although this country has not quite reached their expectations yet they consider the journey one affording great enjoyment. I have heard old soldiers say that this is the most pleasant expedition they have experienced since their first enrollment in the army.

I am told some silver quartz was found today.[74] The country travelled over the past few days is not quite as good for agricultural or stockraising purposes as that travelled over at Camps

---

74. In his journal, Snow claimed that he and Ross made the first gold discovery. On July 27, the two had unsuccessfully prospected a small tributary of Custer Creek above camp. On their return to camp, Ross picked up a small piece of float or blossom quartz; Snow and Ross followed croppings for a mile.

"Gen. Custer," Snow claimed, "had at his own expense, employed two practical prospectors whom I had known for years—J.A. [sic] Ross and Charles [sic] McKay—who were supplied with all necessary tools for prospecting." Ross, McKay, and Snow were messmates and tentmates for the entire expedition.

Making things a bit confusing, though, Snow later wrote: "We encamped in this beautiful valley for three days, and the discovery was made the first day—Aug. 2, 1874— We succeeded in washing out 15¢ to the pan from the grass roots down to a depth of six feet and did not reach bed rock." Snow, "Black Hills Expedition."

18, 19, and 20. There is not sufficient arable land, and the valleys are small.

July 28

The command moved at 5 o'clock. Left the valley and ascended the bluffs. Moved for nearly five (5) miles on fine tableland until we arrived at a jumping off place, where we could not move another step with the wagons. Turned round and came back. Camped about 2 1/2 miles from our last camp. Arrived at Camp No. 24. Marched 10 1/2 miles. Continuation of the same stream which we camped upon yesterday. Grazing good. One horse of E. Co., 7th Cavalry, died from poison.

July 29

This is a hard day's march for the wagon train—Very bad roads. Hard work for the pioneer party. Travelled thro' narrow ravines, timbered hills, steep and stony places. Arriving in the valley encountered four bad crossings. The hills had a beautiful silver appearance, caused by the shining surface of mica.

One artillery carriage broken.

Lieut. Chance, 17th Infy., Officer in charge of Artillery Det., received a kick from a horse ridden by Capt'n French and was badly hurt.

A private of Company C, 7th Cavalry, accidentally wounded in the right arm from a carbine shot. The wagon train did not reach our camp tonight.

Could you hear the profane language which emanated from the lips of some soldiers and civilian employees because they could not reach camp in time to get something to eat you would verily believe that the heathen deity "Hecate, goddess of the lower regions," was let loose.[75] Arrived at Camp No. 25. Marched 14 miles.

---

75. Curtis gives us insight into the character of the soldiers of that period:
"The majority of the enlisted men in the army are simply human driftwood—men who have committed crime elsewhere, and are hiding in the service under assumed

A small creek of good water. Grazing middling. There were 13 deer killed today.

July 30

The wagon train arrived a short time before daylight. Reveille 3:45. The General 6:05. The Command moved at 7 o'clock. Travelled over high rolling prairie—beautiful landscape, picturesque scenery. A more desirable country. Good roads. A wide and open country. A conspicuous hill called Harneys Peak.

If I had the gift of language, or could wield the pen of an able writer it would afford me pleasure in giving a voluminous account of this country with a detailed description of everything pertaining to it, but the reader will observe that in this diary I have followed the course of truth based upon facts, and being young and inexperienced I am unable to give an elaborate narrative. Therefore I hope the critic will deal leniently with me.

The country travelled over today is clothed with rich arable land, capable of producing the cereals, and fruits as cultivated in the Eastern states. This is a fact that can be substantiated by every person accompanying the expedition. Moreover this is a pure atmosphere. The air is salubrious, consequently the health of the command is excellent.

The gentle zephyrs coming from the west, cause mild breezes of aeriform fluid to be sweetly conveyed through the air.

The beautiful hills in this country are inviting in appearance, & though the woodnymph with her many fabled fairies has not been found here in her sylvan glory, yet lofty pines and neat spruce, with a heavy growth of oak has taken her place and proudly demonstrate the fact of an actual existence.

We descended into a beautiful valley. The fruits of the bramble gathered in large quantities. Wild raspberries and gooseberries, currants & cherries seen everywhere on our line of march.

---

names; men who cannot brook the liberties and familiarities of society, and take refuge in military discipline; men who are disappointed, disheartened, and ambitionless, and find the lazy life of a soldier a relief." Curtis declared that Cunningham, the first to die on the expedition, was traveling incognito, and said he believed Turner (shot and killed in an argument) had been doing the same. *Chicago Inter-Ocean*, August 17, 1874.

I am informed that "One Stab" the Indian prisoner guided us to this place. I had nearly forgot this poor captive. The Interpreter tells me that "One Stab" is exceedingly pleased with the treatment received from the Commanding Officer, that he never lived better, and the only thing troubling him is that his relatives suppose he is dead, and are lamenting over his demise. He sincerely hopes when he is restored to freedom that the Ree Scouts may be ignorant of the fact and be prevented from doing him harm.

He is not afraid of the whites, for he has always found them friendly and charitable.

"One Stab" has a son-in-law, a white man who has five children.

Arrived at Camp No. 26. Marched 10 1/2 miles, grazing good, water to be found all around us.[76]

A good Spring of water above our camp.

July 31

Laid over. Companies A & G, 7th Cavalry, divided into four detachments scouted around the country today.[77]

---

76. It was while Custer was in the lead that day (July 30) that he had the opportunity to be what Donaldson labeled "the first civilized man whose eyes beheld this scene of beauty": a natural park over a mile wide—in some places eight miles wide—and fifteen miles long. None had seen anything to equal it. There were expressions of admiration from everyone. Donaldson reported that "after much entreaty, his [Custer's] modesty so far gave way as reluctantly to consent to the request of the topographical engineer that the name be Custer Park."

The prospectors found some evidence of gold in the gravel and sand of the valley. Krause and Olson, *Prelude to Glory*, p. 63; Donaldson, "The Black Hills Expedition," p. 572.

77. July 31 was a day of relaxation for most of the command. Early that morning Custer led a detachment consisting of Forsyth, Ludlow, and the scientific corps toward Harney's Peak; they were escorted by less than a company of cavalry.

While Custer was gone, Major Joseph Tilford, who was the ranking officer in camp, gave a champagne supper under a large tarpaulin stretched under the pine trees. The H Company Glee Club serenaded the party. Ewert observed that "Lt. Col. Fred Grant was one of the party and not the most sober one either."

Wood in his "Reminiscence" made the observation that Grant "was drunk nearly all the time." Wood, Ludlow, Grant, Grinnell, and Ludlow's civilian friend Dana messed together. They had much in common, since they were all about the same age (twenty-five or twenty-six).

August 1

Made a short march of 3 1/2 miles. This change of camp was desirable on account of grazing. Before our view spreads forth a lovely sight. In our front extends one of the most beautiful parks the human eye ever beheld. I have travelled extensively both in Europe and America and I have never seen a more elegant park. Here nature in all her glory has performed a system of created things perfect and wonderful. The ornamental parks and graceful enclosures which I have seen in London, Liverpool, Paris, New York and Philadelphia cannot present such a natural appearance for beauty as this park.[78]

Camp No. 27. Excellent grazing. A large stream of water running through camp.

August 2

Laid over. Companies C & K, 7th Cavalry, accompanied by a det. of Engineers left camp today with three days rations for the purpose of exploring the North fork of the Shyenne River.

The prospectors accompanying the Expedition discovered gold this morning.[79]

Sergeant Charles Windolph told Frazier Hunt (Frazier Hunt and Robert Hunt, *I Fought with Custer* [New York: Charles Scribner's Sons, 1947], p. 38) that Colonel Fred Grant "used to get a little tipsy, but didn't do anybody any harm."

78. Custer named the new campsite Agnes Park to honor his wife's Monroe friend, Agnes Bates, who was her house guest while Custer travelled with the expedition.

79. The question of who discovered gold on this expedition and where he discovered it has been the source of considerable discussion. If Calhoun's diary, with its log, can be considered accurate—and it should be, because Calhoun was in a better position to obtain accurate information and record it properly than was anyone else—then the August 2 date of discovery can be accepted as accurate. There have been some who claimed to have discovered gold earlier, just as there have been some who claimed they were with Custer and survived at the Last Stand.

McKay said gold was first discovered on Gold Run Creek, a tributary of Castle Creek. Jesse Brown and A. M. Willard, *The Black Hill Trails* (Rapid City, S.D.: Rapid City Journal, 1924), p. 39, states: "If this statement be true, it would fix July 27th as the correct date for discovery of gold, for on that day the miners were camped near the headwaters of Castle Creek.... The claim of Ross that he first discovered gold within the corporate limits of Custer City, if in fact he did so claim, would tend to destroy his

August 3

Five (5) companies of cavalry (A, E, F, L & M) and scientific party left camp at 6 o'clock this A. M. under command of Bv't. Maj. General G. A. Custer, U. S. A. for the purpose of exploring the South fork of the Shyenne River. Travelling SW we moved for about twenty-five miles over a very good country. At 2 o'clock we found ourselves marching through an undesirable country barren and destitute of grazing. We were in the saddle for fourteen long hours and it was supposed by our leader and the Engineer Officer that we travelled forty-five miles.

This distance was only guessed at, and it is the opinion of many that we travelled fifty-five miles. On our route struck a large Indian trail—old.

Went into camp within a short distance of Chyenne River near 10 o'clock at night. Water and wood but very little grass to be found.

Charles Reynolds, a government scout, left this point for Fort Laramie with the mail.[80]

---

credibility as to the matter of time and place, for we know that gold was found before Custer camped upon or permitted any of his men to explore the present site of Custer." For additional information, see discussion in John S. McClintock, *Pioneer Days in the Black Hills* (Deadwood, S.D.: Adams Memorial Hall, 1939), pp. 19–22.

In his diary Ewert claims he was, along with Tilford, an eyewitness to the historic event on August 5. This would make Custer's timetable wrong, for by August 5 Charlie Reynolds was well on his way to General Sheridan at Fort Laramie with the dispatch in which the discovery was revealed.

There is also considerable contradiction in the gold discovery stories told by people who were on the expedition, a controversy that is best examined by O'Harra in "Expedition of 1874," pp. 286–98. All agree, however, that gold was first discovered in the Black Hills by Horatio Nelson Ross.

When it came time to post a notice locating claims in Custer's Gulch (the name of the discovery location), Ross was given the fist four hundred feet designated as "Discovery." Claim No. 7 below Discovery belonged to "Aunt Sally," sutler John W. Smith's Negro cook. Sally's real name was Sarah Campbell, a woman that Curtis described as "a huge mountain of dusky flesh."

80.   August 2, 1874
Special Orders
   No. 26
Government scout Charles Reynolds will accompany the five companies of cavalry which leave camp tomorrow morning and at a point hereafter to be designated will proceed with dispatches for Fort Laramie reporting his arrival to the commanding officer of that post.

The Commanding Officer sent the following dispatch:

By telegraph from Laramie or nearest Station

Headq'rs Black Hills Expedition
8 1/2—Eight and one-half miles
Southeast of Harney's Peak:

Assistant Adjutant General
  Department of Dakota

My last dispatch was dated July 15th and sent from Prospect Valley, Dakota. Longitude 103° 46' (one hundred and three degrees and forty-six minutes)—Latitude 45° 29' (Forty-five degrees and twenty-nine minutes). Two of my Indian scouts left as bearers of the dispatch as soon as their departure could be concealed by the darkness.

After leaving that point this expedition moved in a southwesterly direction until it reached the valley of the Little Missouri River, up which we moved twenty-one miles. Finding this valley almost destitute of grazing along our line of march, I ordered the water kegs filled and a supply of wood placed in the wagons, and left the valley in search of a better camp ground.

During our passage up the valley of the Little Missouri we had entered and were about to leave the Territory of Montana. Our course was nearly due south & after a further march of about nine miles before sundown we arrived at a point capable of furnishing us good

On arrival he will deposit in the mail such dispatches and letters as are intended for transmission by mail and should there be a telegraph station at Fort Laramie he will deliver to the operator such dispatches as may be intended for telegraph. Should there be no telegraph at Fort Laramie he will proceed to the nearest telegraph station, taking with him all mail and telegraph matter consigned to his care. On completing this duty he will proceed to Fort Lincoln and await the arrival of this command.

Upon arrival at Fort Laramie he will turn in the public horse ridden by him to the post quartermaster at Fort Laramie, which officer is requested to receipt for same. *Chicago Inter-Ocean*, August 27, 1874.)

Using a compass as his guide, Reynolds spent four nights traveling to Fort Laramie, sleeping in the tall grass each day to keep hidden from the Indians. Libbie Custer later related the hardship and danger he encountered. (Elizabeth B. Custer, *Boots and Saddles*, pp. 240–42.)

Over fifty years after the expedition, Dan Newell, who lived in Sturgis at the time and who had been a blacksmith on the expedition, recalled placing the horseshoes backwards on Reynolds' horse to deceive the Indians into thinking the horse was going in the opposite direction. *Black Hills Weekly* and *Deadwood Telegram*, June 27, 1929.

Snow stated that Reynolds traveled the 150 miles to Fort Laramie with only the stars as his guide, and that the horse's galloping was muffled by putting leather boots on its feet. This seems more reasonable. Snow, "Black Hills Expedition".

grazing and water for our animals, having marched over thirty miles since breaking camp in the morning. From this point to the valley of Belle Fourche we found the country generally barren and uninviting, save in a few isolated places. We reached the "Belle Fourche" on the evening of the 18th of July, encamping where good grass, wood and water were abundant, and at a point a short distance above that marked (15) fifteen on Reynold's map just west of the line separating Dakota from Wyoming. The following day was spent in camp.

On the 20th we crossed the Belle Fourche and began, as it were, skirmishing with the Black Hills. We began by feeling our way carefully along the outlying ranges of hills, seeking a weak point through which we might make our way to the interior. We continued from the time we ascended from the valley of the Belle Fourche to move through a very superior country, covered with the best of grazing and abundance of timber, principally pine, poplar and several varieties of oak. As we advanced, the country skirting the Black Hills to the southward became each day more beautiful. On the evening of the 22nd, we halted and encamped east of and within four miles of the base Inyan Kara.

Desiring to ascend that peak the following day, it being the highest in the western range of the Black Hills, I did not move camp the following day, but taking a small party with me, proceeded to the highest point of this prominent land mark, whose height is given as 6,600 feet. The day was not favorable for obtaining distant views, but I decided on the following morning to move due east and attempt the passage of the Hills.

We experienced considerable delay from fallen timber which lay in our pathway. With this exception, and a very little digging rendered necessary in descending into a valley, the pioneers prepared the way for the teams, and we reached camp by two o'clock, having marched eleven miles. We here found grass, water and wood of the best quality, and in great abundance. On the following day we resumed our march up this valley, which I had explored several miles the preceeding evening, and which led us by an easy ascent almost southeast.

After marching nearly twelve miles, we encamped at an early hour in the same valley. This valley in one respect presented the most wonderful as well as beautiful aspect. Its equal I have never seen, and such too, was the testimony of all who beheld it. In no private or public park have I ever seen such profuse display of flowers. Every step of our march that day was amidst flowers of the most exquisite colors and perfume. So luxuriant in growth were they that men plucked them without dismounting from the saddle. Some belonged to new or unclassified species. It was a strange sight to glance back at the advancing columns of cavalry, and behold the men with beautiful bouquets in their hands, while the headgear of their horses were decorated with wreaths of flowers fit to crown a Queen of May. Deeming it a most fitting appellation, I named this Floral Valley. General Forsyth, at one of our halting places chosen at random, plucked seventeen beautiful flowers belonging to different species, and within a space of twenty feet square. The same evening, while seated at the mess table, one of the officers called attention to the carpet of flowers strewn under our feet, and it was suggested that it be determined how many different flowers could be plucked without leaving our seat at the dinner table. Seven beautiful varieties were thus gathered. Professor Donaldson, the Botanist of the Expedition, estimated the number of flowers in bloom in Floral Valley at fifty, while an equal number of varieties had bloomed, or were yet to bloom. The number of trees, shrubs and grasses was estimated at twenty-five, making the total flora of this valley embrace one hundred and twenty-five species.

Through this beautiful valley meanders a stream of crystal water so cold as to render ice undesirable even at noonday. The temperature to two of the many springs found flowing into it was taken, and ascertained to be 44 and 44 1/2 respectively. The next morning, although loath to leave so enchanting a locality, we continued to ascend this valley until gradually, almost imperceptibly, we discovered that we were on the crest of the western ridge of the Black Hills, and instead of being among barren, rocky peaks as might be supposed, we found ourselves wending our way through a little park, whose natural beauty may well bear comparison with the lovelist portions of Central Park. Favored as we had been in having Floral Valley for our roadway to the crest of the Black Hills, we were scarcely less fortunate in the valley which seemed to rise to meet us in the interior slope. The rippling stream of clear, cold water, the counterpart of that we had ascended the day before, flowed at our feet and pointed out the way before us, while along its banks grew beautiful flowers, surpassed but little in beauty and profusion by their sisters who had greeted us the day before. After advancing down this valley about fourteen miles, our course being almost southeast, we encamped in the midst of grazing whose only fault, if any, was its great luxuriance. Having preceded the main column as usual, with an escort of two companies of cavalry, E and C, and Lieut. Wallace's detachment of scouts, I came upon an Indian campfire still burning and which, with other indications, showed that a small party of Indians had encamped there the previous night, and had evidently left that morning in ignorance of our close proximity. Believing they would not move far, and that a collision might take place at any time unless a friendly understanding was arrived at, I sent my head scout "Bloody Knife" and twenty of his braves to advance a few miles and reconnoitre the valley. This party had been gone but a few minutes when two of Bloody Knife's young men came galloping back and informed me that they had discovered five (5) Indian lodges a few miles down the valley, and that Bloody Knife, as directed, had concealed his party in a wooded ravine where they awaited further orders. Taking "E" company with me, which was afterwards reinforced by the remainder of the scouts and Col. Hart's company, I proceeded to the ravine where Bloody Knife and his party lay concealed, and from the camp beyond obtained a full view of the five Indian lodges, about which a considerable number of ponies were grazing. I was enabled to place my command still nearer to the lodges undiscovered. I then dispatched Agard, the interpreter, with a flag of truce, accompanied by two of our Sioux scouts, to acquaint the occupants of the lodges that we were friendly disposed and desired to communicate with them. To prevent either treachery or flight, I galloped the remaining portion of my advance and surrounded the lodges. This was accomplished almost before they were aware of our presence. I then entered the little village and shook hands with the occupants, assuring them through the interpreter, that they had no cause to fear, as we were not there to molest them. I invited them to visit our camp, and promised presents of flour, sugar and coffee to all who would accept. This invitation was accepted. At the same time, I entered into an agreement with the leading men that they should camp with us a few days, and give us such information concerning the country as we might desire, in return for which service I was to reward them with rations. With this understanding I left them. The entire party numbered twenty-seven. Later in the afternoon, four of the men, including the Chief "One Stab," visited our camp and desired the promised rations, saying the entire party would come up and favor us the following morning as agreed upon. I ordered presents of sugar, coffee and bacon to be given them, and to relieve them of their pretended anxiety for the safety of their village during the night I ordered a party of fifteen of my command to return with them and protect them during the night. But from their great disinclination to wait a few moments, until the party could saddle up, and from the fact that two of the four had already slipped away, I was of the opinion that they were not acting in good faith. In this I was confirmed, when the . . .

Note:
For reasons known only to Calhoun, pages 122 to 128 of his diary were left blank, and Custer's August 2 dispatch to Terry was left incomplete, as is indicated above. The balance of this dispatch, printed in its entirety below, was taken from a fragment of Custer's order and dispatch book in possession of the Western Americana Library, Yale University Library, and from the Forty-third Congress, first session, Senate Executive Document 32, pp. 1-6.

. . . two remaining ones set off at a gallop in the direction of the village. I sent a party of men (scouts) to overtake them and request their return. Not complying with this request, I sent a second party with orders to repeat the request, and if not complied with to take hold of the bridles of their ponies, and lead them back, but to offer no violence. When overtaken by our scouts, one of the two included seized the musket of one of the scouts and endeavored to wrest it from him. Failing in this he released his hold after the scout became dismounted in the struggle, and set off as fast as his pony could carry him, but not before the musket of the scout was discharged. From blood discovered afterward, it was evident that either the Indian or his pony was wounded. I hope that neither was seriously hurt, although the Indians had thus their bad faith as the sole ground for the collision. One Stab, the chief, was brought back to camp. The scouts galloped down the valley to the side of the village, when it was discovered that the entire village had packed up their lodges and fled, and the visit of the four Indians to our camp was not only to obtain rations promised them in return for future services, but to cover the flight of their lodges. I have effected arrangements by which the chief, One Stab, remains with us as a guide three days longer, when he will take his departure and rejoin his band. He claims to belong to both Red Cloud's and Spotted Tail's agencies, but has been to neither for a long time. He has recently returned from the hostile camp on Powder River, and represented that the Indians lost ten killed in their fights with the Bozeman exploring party.

The creek which led us down into the interior of the Black Hills is bordered by bluffs, on the crests of which are located prominent walls of solid rock, presenting here and there the appearances of castles constructed of masonry. From their marked resemblance, I named this stream Castle Creek. The direction of Castle Creek having commenced to lead us more to the northeast than we were prepared to go, and the valley having become uneven and broken, I left this water course and ascended the valley of a small tributary, which again gave us a southeasterly course. After a march of fourteen miles, encamped on a small creek furnishing us an abundance of good water and grass. The direction of this creek was nearly east. On the 30th, moved in the continuation of our previous course, and through a fine open country covered with excellent grazing. After a march of over ten miles, we encamped early in the day, about five miles from the western base of Harney's Peak, finding water, grass and wood abundant, with springs of clear, cold water running through the camp. On the following day the Command remained in camp, except the exploring parties sent out in all directions. With a small party, I proceeded to Harney's Peak, and after great difficulty made the ascent to the crest. We found this to be the highest point in the Black Hills. From the highest point we obtained a view of Bear Butte, in the north part of the plains to the east, far beyond the Cheyenne River. Our party did not reach camp until nearly one o'clock that night, but we were amply repaid for our labor by the magnificance of the view obtained.

While on the highest point we drank the health of the veteran out of compliment to whom the peak was named. On the first of August we moved camp a few miles, simply to obtain new grass, still keeping near the base of the Hills to the east of us. This A. M. I dispatched two companies under Colonel Hart, in a southeasterly direction, to extend our exploration with the South Fork of the Cheyenne River. Tomorrow morning at five o'clock I will set out with five companies of cavalry and endeavor to reach the same stream in a southwesterly direction from Harney's Peak. Reynolds, the scout, who is to carry the dispatches to Fort Laramie, will go with us as far as we go in that direction, then he will set out alone to reach his destination, travelling mainly by night. The country through which we have passed since leaving the Belle Fourche River has been generally open and extremely fertile. The main portion of that passed over since entering the unexplored portion of the Black Hills consists of beautiful parks or valleys, near or through which flows a stream of clear, cold water, perfectly free from alkali, while bounding these parks or valleys is invariably found unlimited supplies of timber, much of it capable of being made into good lumber. In no portion of the United States, not excepting the famous Blue Grass region of Kentucky, have I ever seen grazing superior to that found growing wild in this hitherto unknown region. I know of no portion of our country where nature has done so much to provide homes for husbandmen, and left so little for the latter to do as here.

The open and timbered spaces are so divided that a partly prepared farm of almost any dimensions, from an acre upward, can be found here. Not only is the land cleared, and timber both for fuel and building, conveniently located, with a stream of pure water flowing through its entire length and width, but nature ofttimes seems to have gone further and placed beautiful shrubberies and evergreens in the most desirable locations for building sites, while on Harney's Peak I could contrast the bright green verdure of these lovely parks with the sunburned and dried yellow herbage to be seen on the outer plains. Everything indicates an abundance of moisture within the space enclosed by the Black Hills. The soil is that of a rich garden, and composed of a dark mold of exceedingly fine grain.

We have found the country in many places covered with wild raspberries, both the black and red varieties. Yesterday and today I have feasted on the latter. It is no unusual sight to see hundreds of soldiers gathering wild berries. Nowhere in the States have I tasted cultivated raspberries of equal flavor to these found growing wild here, nor have I ever seen them larger or in greater profusion as I have seen hundreds of acres of them here. Wild strawberries, wild currants, gooseberries, two varieties of pure berries and wild cherries are also found in great profusion and of exceeding pure quality.

Cattle would winter in these valleys without other feeding or shelter than that to be obtained from running at large.

As there are scientific parties accompanying the Expedition who are examining into the mineral resources of the region, the result of whose research will accompany my detailed report, I omit all present reference to that portion of our exploration until the return of the Expedition, except to state what will appear in any event in the public prints, that gold has been found at several places, and it is the belief of those who are giving their attention to the subject that it will be found in paying quantities.

I have upon my table forty or fifty small particles of pure gold, in size averaging that of a small pinhead, and most of it obtained today from one panful of earth.

As we have never remained longer at our camp than one day, it will be readily understood that there is no opportunity to make a satisfactory examination in regard to deposits of valuable minerals.

Veins of lead and strong indications of the existence of silver have been found. Until further examination is made regarding the richness of the deposits of gold, no opinion should be formed. Veins of what the geologists term gold-bearing quartz crop out on almost every hillside.

All existing geological or geographical maps of this region have been found uncorrect. This will not seem surprising when it is remembered that both have been compiled by guesswork and without entering the country attempted to be represented.

The health of my command continues excellent. I will begin my northward march in four days from this date. I do not expect to arrive at Fort Lincoln until the 31st of August.

> G. A. Custer
> Brevet Major General
> Commdg. Expedition

*

10:30 P.M.
August 3rd, 1874

P. S. I left our main camp near Harney's Peak at 6 o'clock this morning with five companies of cavalry, and after a march in a southerly direction of forty-five miles, reached the South Fork of the Cheyenne River at the mouth of a creek flowing from the north and emptying into the Cheyenne midway between the mouths of Flat and Horsehead Creeks.

From this point Reynolds, the scout, sets out in one hour with this dispatch for Fort Laramie.

I reached here at 9 P.M. and will proceed to Harney's Peak by a different route tomorrow morning. The country between here and Harney's Peak is generally open and rolling, and excepting the southern portion, covered with excellent grass.

> G. A. Custer
> Brevet Major General, U. S. A.
> Commdg. Expedition

Note:
Lieutenant James Calhoun's Diary continues:

August 4

Left our camp early this morning and proceeded to Sheyenne River. Arrived at this river at 6 o'clock. Found it to be a beautiful clear stream of water. Took the backward track by a different route. The command suffered for the want of water. In the afternoon, after having marched about thirty miles, reached a point where water, wood and grass were abundant. The greater portion of the country travelled over today is uninviting and not worthy of notice.

Two public horses played out from exhaustion and were abandoned. Saw a signal fire.

August 5

Our march early this morning was over some high hills; rough travelling for man and beast. But we were soon repaid by passing through some fine country. Beautiful parks visible everywhere.[81]

---

81. Reverend S. D. Hinman, who led an expedition from the Spotted Tail Agency on August 5 to seek a more suitable site for the agency, returned with a report of the coun-

At noon we reached the command at camp No. 27, having travelled nearly twenty-five miles. In all, one hundred miles since our departure. Most of our horses had no grain for three days and I can assure you needed rest.

During our absence the soldiers were busy digging for precious treasures. Several members of Co. G, 7th Cavy., obtained some fine rubies. One man of said Company has a ruby in his possession which is a perfect gem.

"One Stab," the Indian prisoner, was released from confinement this P.M., and sent on his way rejoicing to rejoin his band. I am told he was supplied with five (5) days rations. I should like to learn the tale which this Indian tells when he reaches the Indian village.

August 6

The command moved at 5 o'clock. Any quantity of fruit obtained from the bramble. Marched North. Passed several of our old camps and found that our camp fires had burnt the surrounding grass. Travelled through timber for about five miles. General C. killed one (1) deer. Marched 23 1/4 miles. Arrived at Camp No. 28.—rich pasturage. Abundant supply of water from a running stream of pure water.

August 7

Travelled through a rich country—high rolling prairie—good arable land, extensive forests of fine timber, principally pine of large growth. Passed several small valleys with beautiful streams of crystal water running through them.

A large mountain (grizzly) bear was killed late this afternoon. I should judge his weight to be about 600 lbs. The following named persons shot him:

---

tryside that was very different from Custer's report. Parker points out that Hinman's exploration was in the drier southern hills, while Custer had explored the fertile section to the north. Hinman sought the unpleasant; Custer looked for the sunny side of the hills. It was a difference in personalities as well as in geography.

Watson Parker (*Gold in the Black Hills* [Norman, Okla.: University of Oklahoma Press, 1966], pp. 26–27) notes that Custer's statements, in contrast to the spectacular spreads in the newspapers, were cautious regarding gold.

General Custer, USA
Capt. W. Ludlow, Engineer Corps, USA
Private Jno. Noonan, Co. L, 7th Cavalry
Bloody Knife, Indian scout.

Mr. Illingworth, a photographer of St. Paul, Minn., accompanying the Expedition, took a photograph of the hunters on a high knoll behind the tent of the Commanding Officer.

The Indian also killed a Bear.

Abundant supply of wood. In the Black Hills there is no scarcity of timber. Extensive forests of large timber run all through this country, and for this reason I have not mentioned for several days past the fact of wood being found at our camps.

Marched 16 1/2 miles, arrived at Camp No. 29. An excellent stream of water running through camp.

Good grazing.

August 8

We marched by the side of a copious stream of water. We are now travelling in the worst part of the Black Hills, in fact this is the most undesirable portion of country yet moved over.

Dead trees and fallen timber lie across our path. Nothing but huge rocks and concretion of earth welcome our onward march. Notwithstanding right at our feet meanders a beautiful rivulet of rippling water. Several beaver dams. Marched 14 3/4 miles. Arrived at Camp No. 30. Grazing good.

August 9

Marched 7 1/2 miles. Passed by several streams of good water. The country presented the same uninviting appearance as yesterday. A very high hill on our left. General C killed a deer. Arrived at Camp No. 31. Excellent grazing. Camped on a beautiful stream of crystal water. At the headspring of this stream there are two little fountains of cold water rising out of the ground; spurting the icy fluid with great force. Very fine grazing. Though the hills on the right and left are barren, the narrow valley in which we are encamped is clothed with a carpet of rich, wavering grass, luxuriant in growth and excellent in quality.

As we camped at an early hour, after attending to a few little matters, I stepped out of the office tent for the purpose of eliciting information. I had the satisfaction of listening to Mr. Ross inform the Veterinary Surgeon of the regiment that he was perfectly satisfied with the general appearance of this country, and that it was his candid opinion that the many valleys were rich with gold.[82] This person is one of the prospectors accompanying the Expedition, and he is so thoroughly convinced of the wealth contained in this locality that with several others has staked out a claim for future operations. Mr. Barrows, the N. Y. *Tribune* correspondent, informs me that this is the only land in this latitude worthy of publicity, and where the industrious classes can be honestly invited or encouraged to emigrate.

---

82. During 1875, and at the request of Indian Commissioner Edward P. Smith, Walter P. Jenney, a mining engineer, led an expedition to determine the extent of valuable minerals in the hills. Jenney concluded prophetically that "There is gold enough to thoroughly settle and develop the country and, after the placers are exhausted, stock raising will be the great business of the inhabitants, who have a world of wealth in the splendid grazing of this region." See Walter P. Jenney, *The Mineral Wealth, Climate and Rainfall, and Natural Resources of the Black Hills of South Dakota* (Washington, D.C.: Government Printing Office, 1876), p. 56.

In mentioning Jenney's report to him, Indian Commissioner Smith said the report "confirms, in a large degree, the statements of travelers and explorers and the reports of General Custer's military expedition of last year, and shows a gold field with an area of 800 square miles . . . and 3,000 square miles of timber, grazing and arable land of great value for agricultural purposes." Edward P. Smith, *Annual Report for 1875*, p. 8.

Smith's report negated in part the statement he had made in his report the year before: "Exaggerated accounts of rich mines and agricultural lands given in the dispatches of the commander and explorers and correspondents of the expedition intensified the eagerness of the people all along the border to take possession of this country. . . . Notwithstanding the subsequent correction (by Winchell and Hazen) of these exaggerations by statements on reliable information that no indications of mineral wealth were found, and that the lands were undesirable for white settlements . . ." expeditions were fitted out to explore and mine the Black Hills. Ibid., pp. 7–8.

The accounts from the Custer expedition had not been exaggerated, even though many of them had been a bit enthusiastic. (See Forty-third Congress, Second Session, Senate Executive Document 32, p. 5.) According to Annie Tallent, Custer had stated in his report to the War Department: "No discoveries, as far as I am aware, were made of gold deposits in quartz. . . . *Seeking for gold was not one of the objects of the expedition*" (italics added). However, this quote is not with Custer's reports to the War Department that still exist. If Custer made the statement he must have had a loss of memory: he had asked Ross and McKay to accompany the expedition as prospectors. Annie D. Tallent, *The Black Hills* (St. Louis, Mo.: Nixon-Jones Printing Company, 1899), pp. 15–16.

Speaking to several others I find that they look upon these hesperian hills, as vast possessions of intrinsic wealth, capable of insuring enjoyment and rapid prosperity.

August 10

We had a copious shower today. I have omitted to mention the fact that rains are copious and frequent, rendering irrigation unnecessary. There is a constant moisture in the ground, caused by heavy dews, and everything tends to make this a most desirable farming country. Marched 7 1/2 miles, arrived at Camp No. 32, a splendid stream of water running through camp. The engineer Sergeant informs me that this stream is called "Elk Creek." This is the largest stream of water we have reached since travelling through the hills. A cold spring of water behind companies F & L, 7th Cavy. The grazing was not very good.

August 11

Laid over. Companies G and K, 7th Cavalry, sent forward to prepare a road. About 4 o'clock this P. M., Private O'Gara Co. G, 7th Cavy., on duty in the Subsistence Department, returned from hunting and reports the immediate presence of a large body of Indians. The soldier spent the day in washing their clothes and fishing. I saw some very fine fish which were caught in this stream.

The men played the popular game of Base Ball.

August 12

Marched through the timber until we came to an open valley where we went into camp. Marched 5 1/2 miles. Arrived at Camp No. 33. The left wing camped on Elk Creek, the right wing on a beautiful rivulet, running into Elk Creek. This is indeed a delightful place. Excellent grazing. The consummation of real enjoyment. The whole command is in excellent spirits. The soldiers feel that they are fully remunerated for the manual labor performed by them, in beholding such a beautiful country. We were cheered this evening in hearing some good singing by members of Co. H, 7th Cavalry. What a wide contrast to the mournful ditty of the barbarous red men. The songs sung by civilized men are full of inspiration. As these men gave vent to their vocal powers the very hills and dales all awoke, and transmitted the sound through the vast arena of nature. Such melodious notes should soothe the savage breast.

August 13

We did not move camp until 12 o'clock (noon). Travelled through a gap which was found wide enough for a wagon to pass through. This opening in the rocks was a great relief, as many thought we would have to turn back and travel in search of another outlet.

Only marched 4 1/2 miles; arrived at Camp No. 34. Excellent grazing. Water obtained about 400 yards off.

Private (James) King, Co. H, 7th Cavy, died this evening. The members of Company H, 7th Cavy, are exceedingly displeased at the conduct of the Medical officer of the left wing. From what I can glean this subject will be thoroughly investigated on the return of the Expedition. For several reasons, I refrain from saying any more touching this matter.[83]

We are encamped on high tableland with a full view of the open prairie below us.

---

83. Ewert gave an account of this third death on the expedition. According to Ewert, King had fainted twice that day. "The brutes called doctors" continued to mark King for duty until he could not get back on his horse; it was then that he was finally placed in a wagon. The following day (August 13) he died. Apparently King was quite popular with his fellow troopers, and when the news of the events surrounding his death spread among the soldiers, their feelings against "the two inhuman brutes" became evident. Ewert believed that "had an opportunity presented itself they would exact full measure of the devine law 'Eye for an eye, tooth for a tooth and life for life.' "

Ewert expressed himself quite freely about the expedition doctors, and he was equally critical of the expedition officers. He, along with Tilford—who had indicated his dislike for Custer's way of doing things several weeks earlier, presumably because Custer had ordered him to leave his comfortable post at Fort Rice to endure the hardship of the expedition with the other officers of the Seventh Cavalry—objected to King's body being interred that evening, two hours after his death. Ewert probably didn't realize that the night burial was an attempt to prevent Indian desecration. Apparently enough other troopers felt the same way Tilford and Ewert did, so Custer permitted the services to be held the following morning. King was sewn in his tent, wrapped in his blanket, and lowered into his grave while Captain Benteen read the service. Carroll and Frost, *Ewert's Diary*, pp. 70–72.

August 14

Travelled about 4 miles when we got once more on the open prairie. We felt loath to leave the Black Hills. Full well we know that many a time will we wish to be back again in the shady groves of timber and to drink of the pure water which renews the strength and invigorates the body. We are bidding adieu to a country which has been to us a source of real pleasure. Farewell ye lofty hills of western beauty. Farewell ye meadows of verdant pasture. Farewell ye rich valleys and timbered hills. We know that this is the best country that can be found in any of the Northwestern states, and when we move for days upon an open prairie beneath a burning sun, with nothing but warm alkali water to quench our thirst, we will be reminded of the many cold springs of pure water which flowed sweetly from the mountain side, and often will we turn round and cast a wistful desire toward these prominent hills which for many a day afforded us so much enjoyment. We travelled this morning fully 14 miles before we reached water when we arrived at a running stream. By the side of this stream was found three (3) springs hidden from the view by the tall blades of grass. A few miles further we reached Bear Creek which is indeed an excellent and large stream of running water.[84]

While the pioneer company were fixing a crossing the soldiers were busy fishing, a sport which proved satisfaction. I saw one soldier with 21 fish (some of large size) which he caught in about 40 minutes.

---

84. Custer had elected to take a different route homeward because he believed there was little value of traversing country they had already seen when unexplored areas could be surveyed on the return.

At this point the command emerged from the Black Hills. Ewert reported that many of the men in H Company were ill, with ten to fifteen men constantly on the sick report. He states that men were dying (a statement inconsistent with other records), men were getting lost (Bunting, Windolph, and Durfur had been lost for a day while hunting), and horses were giving out. Yet Ewert thought that H Company was better off than the others. Ewert was far from being an optimist; when the march was over and all were safely at Fort Lincoln, he continued to magnify each event of the trail while others considered the expedition to be comparatively easy. Carroll and Frost, *Ewert's Diary*, pp. 72, 82.

In reference to the illness in the command at this point, Forsyth reported in his *Diary* that James King (see footnote 83) had died from typhoid fever. *Chicago Times*, August 27, 1874.

The country travelled over from the outskirt of the hills to Bear Butte was good rolling prairie.

Continued our march north until we arrived near the base of Bear Butte, a prominent landmark worthy of interest.

Marched 26 miles. Camp No. 35 on Bear Butte Creek. Grazing middling; wood & water. The following circular was issued today:

> Headq'rs Black Hills Expedition
> Camp No. 35, D. T.
> August 14th, 1874

Circular No. 25

The command will not move camp to-morrow. A mail will leave this point for Fort Lincoln to-morrow evening. The allowance of mail matter will be three (3) ounces to each company. No mail will be received except between the hours of 5 and 7 P.M. All mail matter from each company will be delivered to the Sergeant Major by a non-commissioned officer of the company.

By order of Brevet Maj. General Custer.

> (signed)   James Calhoun
> 1st Lieut., 7th Cavalry
> A. A. A. G.

*

> Headq'rs Black Hills Expedition
> Camp No. 35, D. T.
> August 14th, 1874

Circular No. 26
Unless notified to the contrary, company Commanders will carry wood and water in the wagons from day to day.

By order of Brevet Maj. Genl. Custer.

> (s'd)   James Calhoun
> 1st Lieut., 7th Cavy.
> A. A. A. G.

August 15

Laid over. Gen'l Forsyth with Company H, 7th Cavy, and scientific party went to Bear Butte and ascended to the summit. I understand Mr. Illingworth the photographer took a picture of this prominent landmark. The Commanding Officer sent a dispatch to Department Headq'rs, a copy of which will be found on page [none given].[85]

6 Indian scouts left with the mail this P.M.[86]

*

Headq'rs Black Hills Expedition
Bear Butte, Dakota
(via Bismarck)
August 15, 1874

Assistant Adjutant General
    Department of Dakota
    St. Paul, Minn.

My last dispatch was written on the 2nd and 3rd instant. I began my return march to our main camp near Harney's Peak, arriving there by

---

85. Custer's letter to Libbie that August 15 disclosed his enthusiasm. He had worked unusually hard to make the expedition a success, and said that he felt he was rewarded because it had "exceeded the most sanguine expectations." Merington, *The Custer Story*, pp. 274–75.

He was proud of having killed his first grizzly bear, and he was equally proud because there had been "no drunkenness, no cardplaying on this trip."

When speaking of the prior misuse of liquor, Custer's reference had been invariably to the officers. He had to depend on them for routine matters and when the going got rough. Since the lives of the enlisted men often were dependent upon an officer's clarity of mind, Custer was alert to any overindulgence in alcohol. Somehow, in writing to Libbie, he had forgotten the quite evident drunkenness of members of the medical corps and, apparently, had elected to overlook Grant's continuous imbibing (see footnote 77).

Though a teetotaler, Custer was not hardnosed about drinking socially. He served wine at dinners in his home, as was the custom at frontier posts, and he would drink water when a toast was offered. He had probably been aware of Tilford's champagne party while he had been away with a detachment on the Harney Peak exploring trip. And surely he saw the photograph of that party Illingworth had taken; which showed Grant in front of a table laden with champagne bottles. Although he tightened discipline on his return, Custer ignored the actual drinking incident because he probably knew that the men needed relaxation.

86. Boston Custer, in a letter to his cousin Emma, indicated that this was to be the last mail. He told her he was riding a mule again, this time to save his horse, since the company expected some hard marching after they left this camp (Camp No. 35). He told Emma that Fred Calhoun, the brother of Lieutenant James Calhoun, "rides a mule for the same purpose." Boston Custer to Emma Reed, 15 August 1874, Colonel Brice C. W. Custer collection.

a different route on the 6th. On the morning of the 7th the Expedition began its march northward, Bear Butte being our next objective point. We advanced without serious obstacle until within ten or twelve miles of Bear Butte, when we found our further progress barred by a high range of impassable hills. We attempted to effect a passage through some one of the many valleys whose watercourses ran directly through the Hills in the desired direction, but in every instance we were led into deep, broken canyons, impassable even to horsemen.

Through one of these I made my way on foot, and from a high point near its mouth obtained a view of the plains outside. Retracing my steps, I placed the command in camp in a fine valley, in which it had halted, and devoted the remainder of the day to a further search for a practicable route through the Hills. The result decided me to follow down a watercourse, which led us first toward the east. This stream proved to be Elk Creek, the valley of which, as well as the stream itself, proved to be at least equal in beauty and extent to any passed through during our march. We camped twice on the stream, and as far as we proceeded its course had a most excellent road; but finding that, like nearly all the streams leaving the hills, its course would take us into a canyon which could be barely made practicable for our wagons. I searched for and discovered a narrow gap in the rocky wall which forms the northern boundary of the valley, and which was conveniently large to allow our wagons to pass through. A march of an hour up a gradual ascent, and through a fine forest, brought us to a beautiful park containing thousands of acres, and from which we obtained a fine view in the distance, of an old acquaintance, the Plains. Here we pitched our tents for the last time in the Black Hills, nearly everyone loath to leave a region which has been found so delightful in almost every respect. Behind us the grass and foliage was clothed in green of the freshness of May. In front of us, as we cast our eyes over the Plains below, we saw nothing but a comparatively parched, dried surface, the sunburnt pasturage of which offered a most uninviting prospect both to horse and rider, when remembering the rich abundance we were leaving behind us. A march of twenty-six miles gradually bearing northward, brought us to the base of Bear Butte, at which point I concluded to remain one day before beginning our return march. I propose to return by a different, although perhaps not shorter, route than that adopted in coming to the Black Hills. I am induced to make this change in order to embrace a larger extent of unexplored country within the limits of our explorations, and particularly to enable us to locate as much as possible of that portion of the Little Missouri of which nothing is now known. I expect the Expedition to reach Fort Lincoln on the 31st of August. The health of the command has been and is excellent. This Expedition entered the Black Hills from the west side, penetrated through the eastern and most southern ranges, explored the major portions of the interior, and passed out through the northeastern ranges which form the boundary of the Black Hills.

From the fact that in all our principal marches through the Black Hills we have taken, without serious obstacle, a heavily laden train of over one hundred wagons, it may be inferred that the Black Hills do not constitute the impenetrable region heretofore represented. In entering the Black Hills from any direction, the most serious, if not the only obstacles, were encountered at once, near the outer base. This probably accounts for the mystery which has long existed regarding the character of the interior.

Exploring parties have contented themselves with marching around the exterior base, and from the forbidding aspect of the Hills as viewed at a distance, inferred that an advance towards the interior would only encounter increased obstacles. In regard to the character of the country enclosed by the Black Hills, I can only repeat what I have stated in previous dispatches.

No portion of the United States can boast of a richer soil better pasturage, purer water (the natural temperature of which in midsummer as it flows from the earth is but twelve degrees above the freezing point), and of greater advantages generally to the farmer or stock raiser than can be found in the Black Hills.

Building stone of the best quality is to be found in inexhaustable quantities; wood for fuel and lumber sufficient for all time to come. Rains are frequent, with no evidence in the country of either drouths or freshets. The season, perhaps, is too short and the nights too cool for corn, but I believe all other grain could be produced in wonderful abundance. Wheat would particularly yield largely.

There is no doubt as to the existence of various minerals throughout the Hills. As this subject has received the special attention of experts who accompany the Expedition, and will be reported upon in detail, I will only mention the fact that iron and plumbago [graphite] have been found and beds of gypsum of apparently inexhaustible extent.

I referred in a former dispatch of the discovery of gold. Subsequent examinations at numerous points confirm and strengthen the fact of the existence of gold in the Black Hills.

On some of the water courses almost every panful of earth produced gold in small, yet paying quantities. Our brief halts and rapid marches prevented anything but a very hasty examination of the country in this respect, but in one place, and the only one within my knowledge where as great a depth was reached, a hole was dug eight feet in depth. The miners report that they found gold among the roots of grass, and from that point to the lowest point reached, gold was found in paying quantities.

It has not required an expert to find gold in the Black Hills, as men without former experience in mining have discovered it at an expense of little time or labor.

As an evidence of the rich pasturage to be found in the region, I can state the fact that my beef herd, after marching upward of six hundred miles, is in better condition than when I started, being now as fat as is consistent with marching conditions. The same may be said of the mules of the wagon train.

The horses of the command are in good working condition. I have never seen so many deer as in the Black Hills. Elk and bear have also been killed.

We have had no collision with hostile Indians.

> G. A. Custer
> Brevet Major General, U. S. A.
> Commanding Expedition.

*

August 16

Saw Indians on the right intercepted by Bloody Knife and Cold Hand, who report that six (6) bands of hostile Indians are encamped on the east side of the Little Missouri awaiting to attack this command on its return march. These Indians, four (4) in number, belong to Chyenne Agency.[87]

Travelled nearly north. At noon arrived at the "Belle Fourche River." The wagons were loaded with wood and water. Our general direction is towards "Slave Butte." Marched 29 1/2

---

87. Ludlow (Reconnaissance, p. 17) said that these four Cheyenne Indians "reported that Sitting Bull, five thousand strong, was preparing to intercept us at the Short Pine Hills." This statement was based on a false rumor spread throughout the companies by an orderly who overheard part of a report made to Custer by two scouts, Goose and Cold-Hand, who had met, unexpectedly, several Sioux families on their way to the Grand River Agency. When the orderly got through mutilating the part of the story he overheard, his repeating it and its retelling through the camp caused considerable excitement and anxiety.

miles. Arrived at Camp No. 36, grazing poor, several holes of alkali water. No wood.

The following circular was issued today:

> Headq'rs Black Hills Expedition
> On the march at Belle Fourche River
> August 16, 1874

Circular [number not given]

Four (4) Indians belonging to Cheyenne Agency intercepted by our
scouts today, report that they left the hostile camp yesterday, and that
six (6) bands of hostile Indians are encamped on the east side of the
Little Missouri, waiting to attack this command on its return march.
Battalion Commanders will keep their commands well in hand, with
flankers well out. No straggling or hunting will be authorized. Too
much care cannot be exercised in picketing camp. Small parties will
not be permitted to march between the advance and head of the train.

By order of Bv't Maj. General Custer

> (signed)   James Calhoun
> 1st Lieut., 7th Cavalry
> A. A. A. G.

*

August 17

We are now travelling over a very barren country—The Engineer Sergt. showed me the famous "Inyan Kara" known as the
highest mountain in the Black Hills. "Terry's Peak" and "Custer's Peak" were also seen in the distance. "Slave Butte," a
prominent land mark, was reached. To our right appeared "Owl
Butte," and on our left were several Buttes called "Deer Ears
and Eyes." Several Indian trails. A signal fire observed. The
grass is sunburnt and of very poor quality & our stock shows
signs of falling away.

Water was found about every six miles. The General killed two
(2) antelope and one (1) rabbit.

Camped on a creek several feet deep containing good water.
Wood in abundant quantity to satisfy all our wants.

Marched 28 1/8 miles. Arrived at Camp No. 37. Grazing indifferent.

August 18

Travelled most of today over a barren country. I am informed the Gen'l killed one (1) antelope and four (4) rabbits. There is nothing worth mentioning in our journey today excepting three (3) prairie buttes which were visible for many miles.

Arrived at Prospect Valley where we encamped going out July 14th and 15th. Time has made a difference in the appearance of this valley. Nothing but burnt grass caused by our camp fires.[88] Through negligence and indolence, the cooks, or those whose duty it was to put the fires out, failed to attend to this matter and hence the scarcity of grass. Proceeding two or three miles farther we arrived at Camp No. 38 which proved to be all that could be desired in this part of the Country. Good water, and grass in abundance. Marched 30 1/4 miles.

August 19

Little Missouri ridges on our left, also some high buttes known as "Little Missouri Buttes." Observed a dense growth of timber in the valley.

Slim Butte on our right. Powder River ridge on our left.

"South Butte" end of Powder River ridge.

Three prominent buttes between short pine ridge and the Little Missouri, noted down as 2 R and S Buttes.

Thirty-five (35) mules played out today.

Several horses abandoned.[89]

---

88. The burned grass may not have resulted from the expedition's untended campfires. Ewert seemed to think that the grass had been burned by the Indians for the purpose of forcing the column to abandon horses or mules that were too weak to travel. After the expedition moved on, the Indians could gather up the abandoned animals and drive them to some little-known pasture to recuperate. Carroll and Frost, *Ewert's Diary*, p. 75.

89. Instead of abandonment, Custer ordered all such stock to be shot. Many of the animals were relieved of their saddles or harnesses and driven along, somewhat like cattle. The troopers called this formation a *Cavee Yard*. (Carroll and Frost, *Ewert's Diary*, p. 76.)

Bad water. Very little green herbage to be found. Marched 35 1/2 miles; arrived at Camp No. 39. Camped on a fork of Grand River. Very little wood, and grazing indifferent. The General killed one (1) antelope today.

August 20

As far as the eye can see the prairie is black with burnt grass. Water obtained about every ten miles. Several men very sick with typhoid dysentery.[90] Marched 30 miles, arrived at Camp No. 40. A good supply of wood. Camped on the bank of the Little Missouri River. Good grazing.

August 21

Laid over today.[91] Serg't [Charles] Stempker, Co. L, 7th Cavy, very sick. The command were ordered to take wood and water in the wagons tomorrow.

---

90. Many of the men had become ill from the burning heat and scarcity of water. When they did obtain water it was muddy, wormy, and extremely alkaline.

On this day the Cavee Yard, according to Ewert, consisted of nearly seventy-five bareback horses and mules. Several animals were shot. Carroll and Frost, *Ewert's Diary*, p. 76.

The following day (August 21) conditions forced the command to lay over and rest their animals.

91. Ewert, in his characteristically pessimistic fashion, estimated that the command would lose "at least a hundred of horses and mules" before they reached the river ford. When the expedition terminated, he concluded that the losses did not exceed fifty but that "the result hardly equal to the value of one of the many horses lost by us and only a success as far as the Custer family is concerned." Carroll and Frost, *Ewert's Diary*, p. 82.

Some horses and mules did not die, but suffered in other ways. Teamster Harry Roberts, in a lax moment, did the unpardonable. Two of his mules got loose in camp and became entangled in the ropes and ties of the headquarters tent. For this Quartermaster Lieutenant Algernon E. Smith ordered Roberts, who was a civilian, to be tied spreadeagle to a wagon for several hours. That position in the hot sun undoubtedly left Roberts with an indelible impression of the rewards for carelessness. Ewert considered this punishment a "vile, mean, flagrant outrage." Ibid, p. 77.

On the other hand, Curtis was highly laudatory of Smith's conduct as the expedition quartermaster. He wrote: "Imagine a man with 1,800 boarders on his hands, and then a livery stable of 1,000 horses and more than as many mules, with a clumsy wagon to every six of the latter. And Quartermaster Smith brought everybody home good-natured." And he brought back every wagon and ambulance intact. *Chicago Inter-Ocean*, September 8, 1874.)

August 22

Came across Gen'l Stanley's trail of 1872.

The General killed 6 ducks and one antelope. Marched 28 1/2 miles. Wood, but very little water. Grazing middling. Camp No. 41.

August 23

The prairie is black all over; no grass (except in isolated spots) to be found for our animals. Our animals are falling away fast. Lt. Chance had some trouble to get his artillery carriages into camp because so many of his horses played out.

The grain which is given to the public animals would be quite sufficient if the grazing was good.

It is the belief of many that the Indians out of pure mischief have set fire to the surrounding grass. Marched 19 1/6 miles. Arrived at Camp No. 42. Very little grass. Camped on Box Elder Creek.

August 24

We travelled over a good country. Fine rolling prairie. If we could have seen this country in June last while the grass was green and everything in full bloom we would have beheld a more beautiful country. Beneath the burnt grass is a rich layer of earth capable of being put in a high state of cultivation.

Passed our trail of last year to the Yellowstone. Marched 24 3/4 miles. Camped on the Headwaters of Heart River. Camp No. 43. Wood and good buffalo grass in a small space close to our encampment.

The Gen'l killed 3 antelope and obtained a porcupine.

August 25

A delightful breeze. Saw Heart Butte.

The General killed four antelope.

Marched 17 1/4 miles. Arrived at Camp No. 44. Wood & water but very little grass. A creek of good water running through camp.

Serg't. Stempker, Company L, 7th Cavy, died to-night.

*

Hdq'rs Black Hills Expedition
August 25, 1874

Col. Tilford

The General directs that you at once turn over your wagon to the Qrmster as it was hauling water for K & H Companies.

He also directs me to say that he considers your allowing your wagon to carry water kegs a direct violation of existing orders on your part and the part of the two Company Commanders.[92]

Respectfully,
James Calhoun
1st Lieut., 7th Cavalry
A. A. A. General

*

August 26

Travelled over a very good country. The grazing in this vicinity last year is noted down as excellent.

We came to the grave of Dan Molloy a teamster who was killed last year by a wagon running over him.

---

92. Tilford, a colonel by brevet, obviously was not a Custer clansman. He had resented leaving his post at Fort Rice for the hardships of an expedition on the plains. Once, while the expedition was in the hills, Tilford had been left in command while Custer went out at the head of an exploration detachment. Immediately, and in contrast to Custer's stringent discipline while the expedition was in hostile country, Tilford loosened the reins on camp discipline, apparently in an effort to popularize himself with the men. Of course, the contrast was even more apparent for the men when Custer returned to command, since all rules and regulations were immediately tightened.

As the column neared Fort Lincoln there was a tendency to loosen up on discipline. Tilford went too far. Water as well as food were under the direct supervision of the quartermaster; Tilford was out of line, and was so advised.

Passed by Heart River where wood and water were put in the wagons. Near a prominent butte I observed a stake of the N. P. R. R. Co. marked 4877; I made a calculation and find we are 92 miles from Lincoln. Arrived at Camp No. 45. Marched 32 1/4 miles. A good stream of water and an abundant supply of wood.

There is every evidence that Indians have camped here recently. It is believed that the party who attacked the Rees at Berthold passed by this way.

The General killed 5 antelope today. The grazing bad.

The remains of the late Sergt. Stempker were interred at tattoo this P.M. Professor Donaldson read the burial service in an impressive manner.

August 27

Marched 17 1/4 miles. Arrived at Camp No. 46. Two springs of cold water. No wood. We have at last reached good grazing. The country before us is clothed with good grass of excellent quality, and no more signs of a burnt prairie. Water and grass in abundance to satisfy all demands.[93]

---

93. This day was an important one for another reason: the August 27 issue of the *Chicago Inter-Ocean* had been a sellout. The story of the gold discovery in the Black Hills was stirring news, and it preempted all other topics of conversation.

Curtis, the *Inter-Ocean* correspondent, knew that Reynolds would carry Custer's report to a postal station to be sent to Sheridan in Chicago (see dispatch included with August 3 entry). When Reynolds left Custer and his detachment on the evening of August 3, Curtis asked him to also carry the stories he had written and to send them over the telegraph wires to the *Inter-Ocean* Chicago office.

Curtis was an unrestrained reporter. Previous stories by other correspondents with the expedition had been conservative in their estimates of gold. It took Curtis to refer to "the precious dust found in the grass under the horses feet." Custer made cautious and conservative statements about gold discovery, and Ludlow suggested that the land should be used for an Indian reservation. None of the other stories stirred up quite as much interest as the almost entire front page story by Curtis. He had been given a lead when an editorial in the August 24 *Inter-Ocean* stated that "it would be a sin against the country and against the world to permit this region, so rich in treasure, to remain unimproved and unoccupied, merely to furnish hunting grounds to savages."

The fanfare and publicity given the gold discovery revived the frontier industry of prospecting. It was a boon to the railroads and was the shot in the arm that frontier business needed.

Excitement ran high. Prospecting parties organized and equipped themselves. As they prepared at Bismarck, Fargo, Sioux Falls, Omaha, Chicago, and many other points to

August 28

The General obtained two (2) porcupines. Marched 16 1/4 miles. Arrived at Camp No. 47. Abundant supply of wood, water and grass.[94]

*

Note:
Calhoun's daily log and diary ends with the August 28 entry. The following correspondence was added by Calhoun after the closing diary entry.

---

the east of the hills, word of these preparations reached Sheridan. The nearest point to the hills—Bismarck—concerned him the most; accordingly, he sent a telegram through Terry to the commandant of the infantry post nearest Bismarck:

St. Paul, Minn.
August 27, 1874

Captain J. D. Poland
6th Infty., Comdg.
Ft. A. Lincoln, D. T.

Please cause an inquiry to be made whether parties are being organized at Bismarck to invade the Sioux Indian reservation with a view of visiting the country known as the Black Hills. If any such parties are found to be forming inform them that they will not be permitted to go unless under authority from the Honorable Secretary of the Interior or from Congress. Report result of inquiry by telegraph. By command of Brigadier General Terry.

Edw. Smith
Capt. 18th Infty.
A. A. A. Genl.

P. H. Sheridan to J. D. Poland, original telegram in Lawrence A. Frost collection.

94. Custer received the following telegram on arrival at Fort Lincoln:

St. Paul, Minn.
August 31, 1874

Lt. Col. G. A. Custer
7th Cavalry
Ft. A. Lincoln, D. T. via Bismarck
The department Commander's annual report has to leave here eighth (8th) September. He desires you to forward at once by mail a brief summary of the operations of your Black Hills Expedition giving all the main features of your formal report which you can forward at your early convenience. Accept the hearty congratulations of the Commanding General for yourself and command upon your success and safe return. Just informed by telegraph that Colonel Sturgis is ordered on recruiting service.

O. D. Greene
Asst. Adjt. Genl.

O. D. Greene to G. A. Custer; original telegram in Lawrence A. Frost collection.

SEVENTH CAVALRY COMMUNICATIONS
1874

Saint Paul, [January] 3rd

Commanding Officer
Fort Lincoln

Lieutenant Hodgson relieved from court. The reduction of civil employees of Quartermasters Department is in execution of peremptory instructions from superior Headquarters and Department Commander has not power to increase your present force.

O. D. Greene[95]
A. A. Gen'l.

*

Rock Island Arsenal, [January] 6th

Col. Custer
Ft. Lincoln

On third instant shipped four thousand horse shoes and fifteen hundred pounds horse shoe nails to Lieut. Nowlan, Fort Lincoln yesterday in obedience to orders from Washington. I changed destination of shoes and nails to Fargo by telegraphing Quartermaster at Omaha. Will hasten transportation as much as I can.

D. W. Flagler
Capt. Ordnance Commg.

*

St. Paul, January 27, 1874

To Commanding Officer
Fort A. Lincoln
Via Bismarck, D. T.

Requisition will at once be made for six hundred (600) sets of horse shoes for your horses. When received here every effort will be made to send them on to Bismarck.

---

95. Major Oliver D. Greene (brevet brigadier general), assistant adjutant general on Terry's staff at St. Paul.

88

Your attention is called to the length of your telegrams. These head-quarters have already been reproved from Division Headqrs. for the excessive use of the telegraph in this command.

O. D. Greene
A. A. G.

*

St. Paul, [February] 8th

Commanding Officer
    Fort Lincoln, D. T.

Direct commanders of companies of cavalry at your post to forward at once requisition for Springfield breech-loading carbines calibre forty-five (45) and Colts revolvers and ammunition for same when shipped; the old ammunition and arms to be transferred to Rock Island Arsenal; furnish copy to Commanding Officer Fort Rice for his information and similar action without delay.

O. D. Greene
A. A. G.

*

Fort Lincoln, March 12th, 1874

The Assistant Adjutant General
    Department of Dakota
    Saint Paul

In deciding upon movement or location of troops for the coming summer I hope the cavalry forces in this section will not be reduced. The present indications being that if hostilities with Indians occur, the brunt will be along this line. The companies here are being constantly reduced by discharges and expiration of enlistments; a division of the force would in view of probable events throw us on the defensive.

(signed)   G. A. Custer
            Bv't. Maj. General, USA

*

89

Fort Abraham Lincoln, D. T.
March 24th, 1874

Assistant Adjutant General
  Department of Dakota
  Saint Paul, Minn.

An advertisement appears in the Bismarck Tribune of 21st inst., calling for contributions of supplies and ammunition to a party of fifty (50) men who purpose to start from here by the middle of next month for the alleged purpose of exploring the Black Hills for minerals. The leader of the party is the keeper of a disreputable house opposite this post. A party of the proposed strength and composition would only invite destruction by the Indians in attempting to carry out the proposed plan.

Besides from the irresponsible character of the leader, and many of the men who are likely to form the party, no good results are to be expected from this projection. While great harm and embarrassment to our relations with the Indians is almost sure to follow. I would respectfully recommend in the interest of all parties that the government through the military authorities give due notice to all persons proposing to engage in the above undertaking—that the proposed movement into the Indian country will not be permitted.

(Signed)   G. A. Custer
                Brevet Maj. General.

*

Headq'rs, Fort Abr'm Lincoln, D. T.
March 28th, 1874

Editor Bismarck Tribune

As the question of organizing an expedition for the purpose of visiting the "Black Hills" country has been discussed in this locality for some time, and as citizens have been taking steps looking to the departure of an expedition, having this object in view I send you herewith a copy of an official telegram this date received from the Commanding General of this military department, which I respectfully request you make public through your columns.

St. Paul, March 28, 1874

Commanding Officer
  Fort A. Lincoln, D. T.

Give full notification in the country around you that the expedition to the "Black Hill" country will not be permitted to invade that region,

90

and that if necessary the military will be employed to prevent it. If nevertheless the expedition prepares to proceed, put your command between it and the country referred to, and report here for further instructions. If after hearing of your notifications the expedition continues to make preparations, inform this office.

                    (signed)   O. D. Greene
                                 A. A. General.

By publishing the above you will confer a favor no doubt upon the parties interested.

I am, very respectfully

                    Yours
                    (s'd)   G. A. Custer
                             Brevet Major General, U. S. Army
                             Commanding.

                                    *

                             Headqrs, Fort Abr"n Lincoln, D. T.
                             April 9, 1874

Assistant Adjutant General
    Department of Dakota
    Saint Paul, Minn.

Hard bread examined, and 80,000 pounds good and fit for use in field this year.

                    (signed)   J. G. Tilford
                                 Commanding Fort Rice

This dispatch was transmitted thro Gen'l Custer.

                                    *

                             Fort A. Lincoln, D. T.
                             April 23rd, 1874

Assistant Adjutant General
    Department of Dakota
    Saint Paul, Minn.

About one o'clock today a band of Indians attacked a party of citizen herders a short distance below this post, and drove off about eighty (80) head of mules belonging to citizens. Within ten minutes after receiving notice of this, I had six companies of cavalry in the saddle, and began a vigorous pursuit, the Indians having several miles the start; for twenty miles we kept up this pursuit almost at a continuous gallop. As the result, I report the recapture of every animal taken by the Indians, and the capture of a portion of the stock belonging to the Indians. I suffered no loss in men while the Indians had at least one of their members wounded, besides being compelled to abandon saddles and other property in their flight. My command behaved handsomely and reached Fort Lincoln on its return at 11 o'clock the same night; no portion of the stock captured by the Indians and recaptured by my command belonged to the government.

(s'd) G. A. Custer
    Brevet Major General, U. S. A.
    Commanding.

*

Fort Abraham Lincoln, D. T.
April 27, 1874

My dear General   .

Since your departure[96] I have been calculating the comparative cost to the government of keeping the ten companies of the 7th Cavalry in garrison or sending them on the proposed reconnaissance. I have estimated the grain and hay allowance to each animal exactly in accordance with that fixed by regulations, the price being that paid for oats, corn and hay at this post. We feed one half oats and one half corn, my calculations cover a train of 100 six-mule wagons, making 600 mules. I also estimate the cavalry horses at 600; from the subjoined figures which are correct it will be seen that my statement made to you last fall that the proposed reconnaissance can be made and result in an actual saving to the government was absolutely correct.

Cost of full grain forage (1/2 corn and 1/2 oats) for 600 horses and 600 mules for one day $313.31. Cost of full hay forage to same animals including bedding allowance $130.00

Total cost per day	$443.31
Cost of 4 lbs grain per animal	
600 horses and 600 mules	$119.35
Amount saved each day on forage	$323.96
Amount saved in 60 days.	$19,437.60

I specify 100 teams for simplicity in figures.

---

96. "Lt. Gen. Sheridan and Gen. Terry visited Ft. Lincoln last Friday (August 24th)." (*Bismarck Tribune*, 29 April 1874.) The *Tribune* noted that Custer promised a visit from Lawrence Barrett, a distinguished Shakespearean actor and intimate friend of Custer's, at an early date.

Take now our increased expenses. The principal of which is pay of teamsters; 100 teamsters at $30 per month cost $3,000.00 and for (2) two months the cost would be $6,000.00; deduct this from $19,434.60 the amount saved on forage and we have $13,437.60. Thirteen thousand four hundred and thirty-seven and 60/100 dollars, in favor of the reconnaissance as a means of economy. This calculation is not based on any idle theory but upon the actual expences as fixed by the regulations, so far as the prices and amounts of forage are concerned.

Yesterday I saw a man who several years ago drove a two-horse train from Fort Pierre (near Fort Sully) to Fort Clark. He kept well out from the Missouri River and I think at a greater distance from the latter than Raynolds route, his wagon carried 1900 lbs; yet he found no difficulty in getting along—except occasionally at the crossings of water courses, the banks being a little abrupt and high; he further states that as he got away from the Mo river the country became higher and more even on the surface—this is in favor of my idea as to following the divide between the Little and Big Missouri rivers. An Indian now at Berthold whom I have sent for today is represented as familiar with the northern portion (at least) of the Black Hills and he states that near the latter the headquarters of the Little Mo and Belle Fourche run within six miles of each other and that he has passed through the Black Hills by a pass practicable or capable of being made so for wagons, somewhere between Bear Butte and Bear Lodge (on Raynolds map), and once through this pass the interior country is of fine quality somewhat like a park. This Indian who I know and believe to be reliable will be here soon, when I will ascertain further.

It will be necessary to embrace the wages of wagon master with those of teamsters, also the wages of an interpreter, as there should be some Indian scouts left at this post and some accompanying the reconnaissance, the latter would also require one interpreter, thus making it necessary to employ one and but one more than now employed.

The party from whom I expect to obtain additional information concerning the Black Hills country will return home Wednesday eve as telegraphed by him. As soon as I have seen him I will let you know the results. It would be well I think as soon as it has become positively determined that this movement is to be made that I should be notified of it in order that I may have as much time as possible to attend to details. I hope you will let me hear from you. Try and send Sandy (Geo. A. Forsyth) and Col. Grant along if I go out.

Truly your friend,
G. A. Custer
Bvt. Maj. General, U. S. A.

*

Headq'rs, Fort A. Lincoln, D. T.
April 30th, 1874

Assistant Adjutant General
    Department of Dakota
    Saint Paul, Minn.

By carrier who left Fort Rice at midnight last night a dispatch is just received from the Indian Agent at Standing Rock, dated yesterday stating that a war party of Indians passed that point the previous night on their way to this vicinity with the object of committing depredations. If they come we will try and be prepared to receive them.

        (s'd)   G. A. Custer
                Brevet Major General, U. S. A.
                Commanding.

*

Saint Paul, May 2, 1874

The Commanding Officer
    Fort Lincoln

Considering all the circumstances of the case the Dept. Commander decides no change can be made in assignment of Dr. Hart. Let him go on by first boat to Fort Shaw.

                O. D. Greene
                A. A. G.

*

St. Paul, May 4th

The Commanding Officer
    Fort Lincoln

The Department Commander desires you to inform yourself at once of the steps taken by Capt. Clarke for recovery of escaped horses and to at once take such additional measures as circumstances may demand. Report action.

        (s'd)   O. D. Greene
                A. A. General.

*

94

St. Paul, May 4th

The Commdg. Officer
    Fort Lincoln
    Via Bismarck

It is now too late to hasten Capt. Grossmann's trial, and the Dept. Commander is not willing to run the risk of it being deferred in consequence of his detail to escort N. B. Survey.

Besides it is not considered to be his turn for the detail[;] designate another company.

                        O. D. Greene
                        A. A. G.

*

St. Paul, May 16th

Release from arrest and return to duty Sergeant Hohmeyer, Company E, 7th Cavalry without awaiting general order in the case acquitted by Court.

                        O. D. Greene
                        A. A. G.

*

St. Paul, May 18, 1874

Lieut Col. G. A. Custer
    Fort Lincoln, D. T.

Orders received for your expedition, authority given to have only eighty (80) teamsters and for not to exceed two (2) months. I can give you the one hundred and ten (110) wagons you wish if you can find the additional teamsters in your command. Gen'l Sheridan says send nine (9) or ten (10) companies.

I will give you ten (10) companies, sending a company from Sully to take care of Rice.

Have you grain enough for the trip, if not tell me how much more you want? What proportions of flour and hard bread will you take? I suppose that you have at Lincoln ten-thousand (10,000) pounds of hard bread and that there are twenty-thousand (20,000) pounds at Rice. DuBarry will ship ten-thousand (10,000) pounds more tomorrow.

How soon do you think it would be well to start out?

Send to me any suggestions which occur to you. Copy of General Sheridan's letter sent you by mail.

(signed)   Alfred H. Terry
Brig. General, USA[97]

*

---

97. Custer had telegraphed Barrett an invitation to accompany him on the Black Hills Expedition. Barrett asked for details and the time table. Custer sent the following reply:

Fort Lincoln, Dakota [Territory]
May 19th, 1874

My Dear Lawrence,

Your letter in quick response to my telegram came in due time and I do not doubt that you have often wondered since "why Custer don't write." Well, as matters have turned out I ought to have written you the same day, and again this morning, my reasons for delay were as follows:

I desired and you wished also that I should inform you of my plans for the summer. I was particularly anxious to do this in order that your plans for visiting me could be made promptly. Now for my delay, I could not write definitely as to my movements so far as duties are concerned until I could hear from General Sheridan, who in turn had to consult with the authorities in Washington. From day to day I have been looking for tidings from General Sheridan until yesterday when the long looked for, long desired telegram came commencing in these words: "orders received for your expedition" etc. etc. concluding with the announcement that particulars would be sent by mail. I now know enough to say when I will start and when return as both these dates are under my control. I have telegraphed that we will start not later than the 15th of June, depending on the conditions of the grass. I will be absent from this point not to exceed two months. Therefore, if we set out from here on or before the 15th of June, our return would be on or before the 15th of August. From your letter in which you give the date of termination of present session 5th of June and the date at which you must commence preparations for fall campaign, I am not encouraged as to the prospect of receiving the long expected visit unless you can arrange to be absent for two months commencing June 15th. It is one of those propositions which cannot be considered except by wholesale for the reason that we wave our adieux to Fort Lincoln on the 15th of June, we bid adieux to civilization and civilized beings until our final return and plunge into regions hitherto unvisited by white men.

If you could or can tear yourself away from your business engagements long enough to accompany us, I feel assured it would do more to renew and strengthen your energies physical and mental than anything you might do. You would return a new man and feel as if you had really been drinking the true elixir of life. The expedition in [sic] entirely peaceful in its object, it being the intention to explore the country known as the Black Hills and gain some knowledge as to the nature of the latter. For many years it has been believed from statements made by Indians that the Black Hills are rich in minerals. It is well known that we will pass through the best game region in this country—elk, deer, antelope, grizzly bear and cinnamon bear, beaver and other smaller animals.

I say that our object is a peaceful one but I have no idea that our trip will be so. The Indians have long opposed all efforts of white men to enter the Black Hills and I feel confident that the Sioux will combine their entire strength and endeavor to oppose our progress. I will have a well equipped force, however, strong enough to take care of itself

Fort Lincoln, D. T.
May 18th, 1874

Assistant Adjutant General
Department of Dakota

To fill the six companies of cavalry of my command to their maximum strength ninety recruits are required. The Rice companies at this rate would require sixty recruits, making an increase to the force of the expedition of one hundred and fifty men. I believe I will require all the available strength of the ten companies for service on the proposed expedition, and if possible to obtain recruits before starting I would

---

and of its friends who will honor us by their presence. I will have ten full companies of the best cavalry in Uncle Sam's service, a detachment of Indian scouts taken from bands friendly to the whites and hostile to the Sioux, and a section of Gatling guns, the latter capable of being fired fifty times a minute. I will tell you candidly that we will have contests with the noble red man but my friend, Lawrence, need feel no anxiety on that score as he can remain an impartial observer of the battle and be exposed to no danger whatever.

The trip will be deeply interesting from many courses. We expect to discover a rich and valuable country. The Indians described the scenery as wonderfully interesting and beautiful. One portion of it is named by them "the country of the long bones" from the fact that the land is filled wih numerous petrifications of animals from the description of which must have belonged to a species larger than any now inhabiting this country.

There will be a very pleasant party of officers in my command. I also expect Col. Fred Grant and Gen. Forsyth of Sheridan's staff to report to me for duty during the expedition. Our marches will be made leisurely and will not be fatiguing. We all look forward to it as *the* expedition. General Sheridan, who visited me a couple of weeks ago to confer as to the details of the movement, says it will be the most interesting expedition since the war.

Now Lawrence, I have stated all the conditions. I would not ask or expect you to put yourself in danger. I believe in every man following his legitimate calling. Yours is neither to kill or to be killed by Indians and if there is any of this work to be done, you can remain a spectator under circumstances involving no personal danger. We will receive no mails while absent but I hope by means of my Indian scouts in whom I have every confidence, to send letters back probably once a week. The scouts will have to travel under cover of night and conceal themselves during the day.

Now if you can possibly absent yourself from your duties during the two months referred to, come and go with us and you will never regret it. I have a comfortable large tent of which I will be the sole occupant unless you are my companion.

You shall taste of greater varieties of game than a New Yorker has ever dreamed of and it will not be such as you obtain in the market houses sometimes of doubtful condition, but it will be of such delicious flavor and condition as will make you wonder if you ever really tasted game before. Your mount shall be such Murat himself would envy you. The appetite you will have for food and the soundness of your sleep will be so different from those usually enjoyed by professional gentlemen in all kinds of life, that you will think you have fallen into fairyland and when you return to the states you will feel like a man who has been granted a renewed lease of life. This is no fancy sketch but is proven by the experience of hundreds of my companions.

Now then, can you not arrange your affairs so that you can devote two months to health, pleasure and a different life? The outfit you will require will be of the simplest

strongly urge it. I desire also to take the maximum number of wagons indicated in despatch of Department Commander yesterday, and to do so will be compelled to weaken correspondingly my fighting force in order to supply teamsters above allowance of citizens. An application for recruits would probably be granted under the circumstances.

(signed)   G. A. Custer
Lieut. Colonel, 7th Cavalry.

*

Fort Abr'm Lincoln, D. T.
May 19, 1874

General Terry
Saint Paul

Your dispatch received. Information you desired regarding grain and bread sent today. I have not conferred with Tilford but presume it will

---

and plainest material. You will feel it a splendid place to wear out old clothes. You will require three or four colored shirts. Most of our officers wear a blue flannel shirt trimmed with white braid, something like a Navy shirt. On ordinarily warm days we wear no coats but ride in our shirt sleeves. It is the freest, easiest sort of life one can imagine. I generally wear buckskin coat and pants winter and summer. You will not require but few changes, your pants and boots should be made with reference to riding. You will require no arms. I can furnish you anything required in that line from a ten pounder to a hunting knife. You will also require one India rubber overcoat and overalls for wet weather, a broad brimmed slouch hat, a couple of comfortable blankets. I could furnish you blankets in abundance, but the quality would not be satisfactory perhaps. It is, however, such as we use. Your outfit would not cost you but a few dollars—less than the price of one weeks board at a hotel. Your expenses will be those incurred in travelling by rail to and from this point.

If you can find any stores or hotel or other places to spend money from the time you leave this point until we return, you will be a greater discoverer than Livingston. Now my dear boy, see if you cannot arrange to join us. You will never regret it, I am sure, and I know I would enjoy your visit more than language can express. Write me at once and give me your decision. I am in the midst of busy preparations for the march this will account for the absence from this epistle of reference to affairs generally. We are all well and have had a delightfully pleasant winter in all respects. It seemed so hard to have you and Mrs. Barrett come so far west and yet not reach us. We must surely meet when your fall engagement commences. I speak now of thee and thine and me and mine. As for you, I will continue to hope that the fates will so arrange it that I may welcome you the comradeship of my camp and cot during my ramble to the Black Hills.

I must say adieux for the present. Much love to Mrs. Barrett and yourself from Mrs. Custer and her better half. Write to me soon and say "I'm coming."

Truly your sincere friend,
Custer

George A. Custer to Lawrence Barrett, Manuscript Division, Library of Congress, Washington, D.C.

be agreeable to him, and I would suggest that in order to give me control over equipment and preparation of the four companies at Rice for the field, and to get the benefit of such stores there as may not be required for the four companies, that I be given a temporary control of that post say until the expedition moves out. I merely make this as a suggestion. I desire to obtain two of the four Gatling guns now at Rice.

(signed)   G. A. Custer
Lieut. Colonel, 7th Cavalry.

*

Headq'rs, Fort A. Lincoln, D. T.
May 19th, 1874

Assistant Adjutant General
  Department of Dakota
  Saint Paul, Minn.

I will require (200,000) two hundred thousand pounds of grain and to economize transportation would prefer all corn instead of mixed oats and corn. I propose to take one-third flour; two-thirds hard bread. If vegetation advances as at present I think the grass will enable me to start by the 15th of June at the latest. I would like if the Depot Quartermaster at Yankton could be instructed to employ Major Lyman as wagonmaster and send him here by first steamer. He is a most competent man in that position, was with me last summer and would be invaluable on the proposed expedition. He resides in Yankton. I desire to call particular attention to the failure of the forwarding officers to send to this post the ordnance stores including arms and ammunition required for, invoices of which have been received as long ago as in December. We cannot move without these stores. The invoices state that they were sent care of Depot Q'rmaster at Omaha. I desire, and all the company commanders concur in the desire to obtain revolvers for this command, Smith & Wesson's or Colt's improved pattern preferred. Four-fifths of our carbines are unserviceable, hence the importance of tracing up the stores enroute.

Please telegraph me if we can obtain revolvers.

(signed)   G. A. Custer
Bv't Maj. General, USA

*

Fort Lincoln, D. T.
May 19th, 1874

General Terry
Saint Paul

I would strongly advise against sending two or three companies on the proposed reconnaissance of the route I will take for the reason that I have obtained what I deem perfectly satisfactory and complete information regarding the route I will follow. I have enlisted within the past few days scouts who are entirely familiar with every foot of the route from here to and beyond the Black Hills, giving every water course on the route. To verify this information I sent to Standing Rock Agency and induced some Sioux to visit me who have hunted between here and the Black Hills every year. These Sioux confirm the accounts I previously obtained from the scouts enlisted by me; I feel entirely satisfied with the information thus obtained and deem it trustworthy in the fullest degree. If you will draw a straight line from this point to Slim Butte, and another line from Slim Butte to Bear Butte, it will almost indicate the proposed route. This will carry us across the numerous small streams which go to make up the tributaries of the Missouri and Little Missouri. It is represented by both the Scouts and the Sioux referred to, that I will not be called upon to make any march exceeding fifteen miles without water, and that the country is beautiful for travelling over, being at no point between here and Bear Butte as abrupt and rolling as that in the immediate vicinity of Lincoln.

Neither the companies here or at Rice are prepared to leave their garrisons yet for various reasons; they are in the midst of busy preparations for the field. They are all greatly deficient in arms, those on hand having been generally condemned while new ones are expected daily. We have neither lariats, nor other facilities for securing our horses in camp, all these articles being expected daily. I am strongly of the opinion that every day of the time between this date, and the date of departure of the expedition can be most profitably spent in preparation. I am exercising my men daily at target practice with the few serviceable arms on hand, and I find they need this practice very much. If the Division Commander could come to St. Paul and I proceed there with two or three of the Indians referred to, I think their statements would satisfy him that I will encounter no difficulty on the proposed route. If however the reconnaissance indicated in your telegram today is still desired I will lose no time in carrying out the order into execution.

(signed)   G. A. Custer
Lieut. Col. 7th Cavalry
Commanding
*

100

Fort A. Lincoln, D. T.
May 20th, 1874

Assistant Adjutant General
   Department of Dakota
   Saint Paul, Minn.

Lieutenant Chance is here on brief leave of absence from Grand River; there are two (2) additional officers with his company. He desires active service and I request that he be assigned to temporary duty with my command for service in the field. I have but one company with more than one officer with it, and I desire to place an officer in charge of Gatling guns which the Department Commander verbally authorized me to take in the field. Lieutenant Chance has had considerable practice with these guns and I would assign him to that duty. He informs me that the Captain of his company gave him hearty approval in this matter.

Please telegraph reply.

(s'd)   G. A. Custer
Lt. Col., 7 Cavy.

*

Saint Paul, Minn.
May 20, 1874

Lieut. Colonel G. A. Custer
   Commander
   Fort A. Lincoln

Gen. Sheridan desires that two or three companies of cavalry be sent out in advance to make a reconnaissance on the route of your intended expedition for a distance of about a hundred miles. He thinks that you may in this way obtain information which will be valuable to you. I suppose that you can make it in six or eight days—you can take companies from Lincoln or Rice for this purpose.

Telegraph me when you think you can start them out and I will send orders.

Alfred H. Terry

*

101

St. Paul, May 22nd.

Gen. G. A. Custer
    Fort Lincoln

Lymon positively declines to go. Can you secure a satisfactory wagon-master at Lincoln.

Benj. C. Card
C. Q. M.

*

Fort A. Lincoln, D. T.
May 22, 1874

Assistant Adjutant General
    Department of Dakota

In view of the number of troops to take the field under my command, I hope it will be deemed proper and practicable by the Department Commander to assign a commissioned officer of the Medical Department for duty with the Expedition. I should be pleased if Asst. Surgeon Kimball could thus be assigned. I make this application from having seen how efficient he is in the field, and from a knowledge that he has written a private letter to a medical officer of this post expressing a desire to accompany the Expedition. If his services cannot be obtained, and Asst. Surgeon Cowes is willing to accept the detail, I would suggest his name doing so with due regard to the interest of science, apart from his professional ability.

(s'd)   G. A. Custer
         L't. Colonel, 7th Cavalry

*

Fort A. Lincoln, D. T.
May 23rd, 1874

General Card
    Chief Quartermaster.
    Department of Dakota

I can obtain an excellent wagonmaster here.

(s'd)   G. A. Custer
         Lieut. Colonel, 7th Cavalry

*

102

Fort Abraham Lincoln, D. T.
May 23rd, 1874

General Terry
   Saint Paul.

After considering the matter I prefer to take the full number of wagons you specified in your telegram, although to furnish the extra teamsters will draw heavily on my command and compel me to rob Peter to pay Paul. If the infantry could be spared I would ask for at least two companies to go. This would not add to the expense. I have conversed with two delegations of reservation Indians and in this way as well as from other indications which I will give you more fully by letter I am satisfied that the Indians do not intend to strew flowers on our path way.

I can go and return with the force I have but two companies of infantry with their Springfield guns would be a powerful support. I send this as a semi-official suggestion for your consideration. Would like your reply. One hundred and ten wagons requires thirty additional teamsters, almost equalling to the fighting strength of a company. I do not desire the infantry as teamsters. I hope Ludlow will be sent with me. He should bring with him an experienced topographer.

(s'd)   G. A. Custer
Lieut. Colonel, 7th Cavalry[98]

*

---

98.   Headquarters Military Division of the Missouri
Chicago, Illinois, May 25th, 1874

Colonel W. D. Whipple
   Asst. Adjt. Gen., Hdq. of the Artry.
   Washington, D.C.

Colonel,

    It appears from a communication from Lieut. Col. Custer, 7th Cavalry, that I misunderstood him in reference to the probable cost of the employes [sic] of the expedition to the Black Hills, and that, while it would be economy to the extent of some $13,000 to send out the expedition, still it would cost about five or six thousand dollars for the lure of the necessary teamsters, wagonmasters and scouts, giving sixty days as the highest limit of absence. I have reduced this amount to the figures of about $5,000 say, for sixty days out, and we will want about $2,500 more than that sent. The fund will not be needed until after the commencement of the fiscal Year.

    The expedition will examine a country heretofore unknown, and for the ultimate object of establishing a military post in the Black Hills, on or about the western line of the Sioux Reservation, which seemed to meet the approval of the Secretary of the Interior

103

Fort Abraham Lincoln, D. T.
May 26th, 1874

Assistant Adjutant General
Department of Dakota
Saint Paul

"Two Bears" reports to Tilford that one hundred warriors left Cheyenne Agency, to attack this place. They were to encamp on Cannon Ball last night. I hardly think they will come here, if they do we will be prepared. Tilford's Scout reached here at two o'clock this morning.

(signed)   G. A. Custer[99]

*

at a consultation last fall in Washington, when the President, Gen. Sherman and the Secretary of War were present.

Yours truly,
P. H. Sheridan
Lieut. General

P. H. Sheridan to W. D. Whipple, Letters Received, Office of the Adjutant General, Roll 152, National Archives, Washington, D.C.

99. The *Chicago Inter-Ocean* (1 July 1874) reported that powerful Sioux war parties had abandoned their reservations for the purpose of attacking the Rees. The opinion was expressed that "what these Sioux tribes want most is such a defeat as will require considerable burying after it."

Sheridan's headquarters released to the *Inter-Ocean* Custer's dispatch of May 26, which indicated that the pretext of attacking the Rees was a subterfuge. It was believed that not only would the Sioux attack the Rees as in the past, but would also give vent to their hostility on all of the whites along the frontier. The following dispatch was sent in reference to the situation:

Headquarters Department of Dakota
St. Paul, Minn., May 26, 1874

General G. A. Custer
Fort Abraham Lincoln, D. T.
Via Bismarck

Your dispatch received. Dispatch just received from General Sheridan says, Tell Custer to lay close for the party of Sioux on its way to attack the Rees. The Rees and Mandans should be protected same as white settlers. If you think it advisable, delay your visit here till you can settle this matter. A chance to put an end to these forays of the Sioux may be more important even than your expedition and at any rate the expedition will not suffer by a few days delay in starting. Answer.

(Sgd.)   Alfred H. Terry
Brig. General, U. S. Army

Alfred H. Terry to George A. Custer, Letters Received, Office of the Adjutant General, Roll 152, National Archives, Washington, D.C.

St. Paul, May 28, 1874

Gen'l G. A. Custer
  Fort Lincoln

Dispatches of yesterday to Col. Greene and myself received. You can retain General Carlin for the present.

Your plans are all right but you must be entirely satisfied that the movement means active hostility before acting. If however hostility is manifest against either of the posts while settlers or peaceable Indians living under the protection of the government make your blow sharp and decisive.

The two blacksmiths are authorized. Gen. Stanley has today been ordered by telegraph to send at once to Rice one (1) company of infantry from Sully and one from Grand River.

Alfred H. Terry
Brig. General, U. S. A.

*

St. Paul, May 29th, 1874

Lieut. Col. G. A. Custer
  Commdg. Fort Lincoln

Dispatches received. I think you are right about the necessity of infantry as a train guard and if it can be done without adding to the expense of your expedition I will give you two (2) companies.

We will settle the matter when you come down.

Alfred H. Terry
Brig. General
Commanding.

*

Fort Abraham Lincoln, D. T.
May 29th, 1874

General Terry
  Saint Paul, Minn.

General Stanley writes me that some of the young Officers of the 22nd Infantry would like to go with me this summer. If their companies are not to take the field and as I have but one officer to a company perhaps an arrangement could be made by which these Officers could be made available with the Expedition. I think it would be satisfactory all around.

How about a medical Officer?

(signed)   G. A. Custer
Brevet Major General, U. S. A.

*

Fort Abr'm Lincoln, D. T.
May 29th, 1874

General Stanley
  Fort Sully, D. T.

I sent a reconnaissance from Fort Rice to examine Cannon Ball for trail of war party; the reconnaissance returned at one p. m. today having proceeded as far as a point due south from Dog Teeth Butte. No signs of Indians were discovered except one moccasin track two days old.

The reconnoitering party marched eighty miles. I should not be surprised if the war party had gone to join the hostile camp for operating the coming summer.

I would like your opinion on this point. Also if the chiefs or agent have received any later informations as to directions taken by war party. Can I obtain either of the young half-breeds John or George as interpreter. Bloody Knife is with me and speaks Sioux and Ree.[100] Do

---

100. Bloody Knife had a Sioux father and an Arikara (Ree) mother. Acting as Custer's chief scout, he and Lean Bear were the leaders of the following Ree Scouts:

Bear's Ears	Two Blackfoot
Horns-in-Front	Standing Soldier
Crow Bear	Standing
Young Hawk	Red Horse
Red Bear	Bear's Arms
Little Sioux	Strikes Two
Bear's Eyes	Bear's Belly
Left Hand (there were two	Enemy Heart
scouts by this name)	Goose
Elk Face	Spotted Horse Eagle
Angry Bull	Shoots the Bear
Angry Bear	Crooked Horn
Red Angry Bear	

Twenty-five Santees also acted as scouts. Orin Grant Libby: *The Arikara Narrative,* North Dakota Historical Collections, vol. 6, (Bismarck, N.D.: North Dakota Historical Society, 1920).

not the Santees know the Black Hill country well and could those we obtained last year be obtained. I would be very glad to have the services of some of your young officers as proposed.

Can you not assign them.

> (s'd)   G. A. Custer
> Lieut. Colonel, 7th Cavalry.

*

> Fort A. Lincoln, D. T.
> May 30th, 1874

Assistant Adjutant General
Department of Dakota

I can only count up the following wagons as available
  30. Thirty from Lincoln
  35. Thirty-five from Abercrombie
  15. Fifteen from Rice
  5. Five from Sully
  10. Ten to be fitted up here from the (48) forty-eight extra mules, and (10) ten extra wagons from Abercrombie.

If Rice can be furnished with forty-eight (48) single sets lead harness the number from them can be increased to (23) twenty-three complete wagons and teams.

By making some repairs Rice can increase the number of wagons without mules or harness to (35) thirty-five or more.

> (s'd)   G. A. Custer
> Brevet Major General, U. S. A.

*

> Saint Paul, May 30th, 1874

Lieut. Col. G. A. Custer
  Commdg.
  Fort Lincoln.

Referring to your telegram relative to detail of infantry officers, directions will be given that the two infantry companies which go with the expedition have full complement of officers.

This is all that can be done. Doctors Williams and Davis will accompany the expedition.

E. M. Smith
Capt., 18th Infantry
A. D. C. P.

*

Fort Lincoln, D. T.
May 30, 1874

General Terry

The report relating to organization of armed expedition at Bismarck is an idle newspaper statement.[101] The alleged organizer of the expedition saw report and wrote me a letter stating he had never entertained any idea of organizing an expedition contrary to the wishes of the government. It was seriously proposed some time ago but the public notice given by telegraphic authority from Department Headq'rs forbidding an expedition to the Black Hills caused the idea to be abandoned. From the failure of the war party which left Cheyenne Agency to put in an appearance up to this time, I am inclined to adopt the idea ad-

---

101. The *Bismarck Tribune* had taken on Chamber of Commerce-like promotional responsibilities ever since Hazen and Custer had begun their entanglement. The *Tribune* encouraged Custer (who needed little encouragement, since it was his custom to see all topography through rose-colored glasses) to speak rapturously of the land over which the Northern Pacific Railroad was to traverse.

Other newspaper accounts were published. The public was becoming excited with reports of gold in the Black Hills. The May 27 issue of the *Tribune* headed a column *TWO EXPEDITIONS! GOLD! GOLD!,* and then proceeded to describe the preparations being made in Bismarck for an expedition of seventy-five to one hundred men organized by the redoubtable Chris. Gilson "for the purpose of seeking gold in the Black Hills." The newspaper account continued: "For some 18 years Chris. Gilson has operated on the western plains, now a guide and interpreter, then occupying positions of higher trust.

"For years he has been an attache of the 7th Cavalry—a sort of nephew of the regiment, but of late, Chris has chosen to take his own course, and in this case he not only proposes to go independent of the 7th Cavalry, but in spite of it."

The newspaper column indicated that the Seventh Cavalry would leave about June 15 on a peaceful mission into the Black Hills; the writer encouraged private expeditions into the Hills.

Terry soon learned of Gilson's proposed expedition and responded by telegraphing Custer on May 30: "Extract from Bismarck papers published here say that armed Expedition is organizing at Bismarck to go to the Black Hills. Please ascertain and report as to the truth of this statement." Alfred H. Terry to George A. Custer, original telegram in Lawrence A. Frost collection.

The *Tribune* published a notice in its June 3 issue that Gilson's expedition had been stopped by the military authorities.

vanced by some of my scouts that the war party has either gone to the hostile camp to unite in operations during the summer or has gone to the Little Missouri to strike the hunting parties from the Gros Ventres, Mandans, and Rees which are known to frequent that stream at this season of the year. I have sent some of my scouts to examine Heart River for trails a distance of thirty or forty miles. Should they fail to discover any signs I will doubt the propriety of a combined or extended movement with the cavalry from here and Rice in search of the war party, particularly as it can now do no serious harm at Berthold as the agent writes me thanking me for the warning, and says they will be prepared to give the war party a warm reception should it appear. The time which would be employed, say eight or ten days, would be very valuable for the expedition. Is there no way by which the services of a geologist can be had with the expedition?

The country to be visited is so new and believed to be so interesting that it will be a pity not to improve to the fullest degree the opportunity to determine all that is possible of its character scientific and otherwise.

(signed)   G. A. Custer
Brevet Major General, U. S. A.

*

St. Paul, May 31st, 1874

General G. A. Custer
Fort Lincoln

New revolvers for your ten (10) companies with ammunition were to be shipped from Rock Island Arsenal yesterday via St Paul. I am trying to get new carbines also.

Alfred H. Terry
Brig. General, U. S. A.

*

Fort Lincoln, D. T.
June 2nd, 1874

General Terry.
Saint Paul.

I do not know any one thing which would add more to the confidence of my command than the new carbines. I will leave here for St. Paul Thursday morning.

(signed)   G. A. Custer
Lieut. Colonel, 7th Cavalry.

*

Fort Lincoln Via Bismarck, D. T.
6/6/74

General G. A. Custer

Headq'rs Dep't of Dakota, St. Paul. Forty (40) teamsters are transferred from Abercrombie; twenty-five (25) can be procured here; balance should be sent. Two (2) wagonmasters and four (4) assistants at least should be authorized. They can be procured here.

G. B. Dandy
A. Q. M.

*

Fort Lincoln via Bismarck, D. T.
6/6/74

General Custer
St. Paul, Minn.

Can get about thirty-five (35) teamsters here. Have telegraphed Gen'l Card on subject. Please get eighteen (18) new wagon saddles for outfit.

G. B. Dandy
A. Q. M.

*

Chicago, Ill., 6/8/74
St. Paul, Minn.

To General G. A. Custer
U. S. A., St. Paul, Minn.

Your telegram received. I had authorized additional teamsters before receipt of your despatch. I had also telegraphed about new carbines, but as yet received no answer.

(signed)   P. H. Sheridan
Lt. General

*

Fort Sully, D. T.
June 8th, 1874

To General George A. Custer
Fort Lincoln, D. T.

Capt. Irvine's Company will be at Fort Rice on the twentieth (20th) inst. He has three (3) six-mule teams and wagons which you are to retain for your expedition. The escort and drivers to be sent down by first boat. I will start with two (2) additional six (6) mule-wagons and teams day after tomorrow, the drivers and escort to return by boat. L. F. Casey will be up with Capt. Irvine's Company. He wants to go with you. I have notified Headq'rs. If you want him apply to Gen. Terry. Who is to be your Quartermaster? Have you heard anything of the war party which left here; very few turned back? Please have your Quartermaster mark our teams so we may get the same ones back. Shall the teams and wagons be invoiced? It is best they should be. I telegraphed to Rev. S. A. Hinman, Springfield, D. T., for you the same Santee Scouts I had last year. I told him to telegraph you; have you heard from him? Send orders to Fort Rice to retain the three (3) teams with Irvine's company.

D. S. Stanley
Colonel, 22nd Infantry.

*

Fort Lincoln, D. T.
June 11th, 1874

Dr. Williams recommends Acting Assistant Surgeons Allen & Porter for assignment to duty with expedition in which I concur if their present places can be supplied. Dr. Allen desires the detail, I cannot speak for Dr. Porter.

(signed)   G. A. Custer
Brevet Major General, U. S. A.

*

Fort Lincoln, D. T.
June 12th, 1874

General Card
Saint Paul

Dr. Williams from Fort Rice reports that the ambulances at Fort Rice are unserviceable, and probably can not be made serviceable for expe-

111

dition. Should this be true will it be practicable to replace them? I understand there were several new ones brought back by Yellowstone Expedition last fall, one serviceable now at Camp Hancock.

(s'd) G. A. Custer
Brevet Major General, U. S. A.

*

Yankton Agency, D. T. 6/12/74

To General Custer
Fort Lincoln

The Santee Scouts will go. Advise me where and to whom they are to report. Answer to Springfield, Dakota.

Samuel D. Harriman

*

Fort Lincoln, D. T.
June 12th, 1874

Assistant Adjutant General
Department of Dakota

The services of a hospital steward are requested with the expedition, and none available for this detail at this post.

(s'd) G. A. Custer
Brevet Major General, U. S. A.

*

Fort Lincoln, D. T.
June 12th, 1874

General D. S. Stanley
Fort Sully

No news from war party—I think they have united with hostile camp for operations this summer. Can I get a Sioux interpreter—George or John preferred? Lieut. Smith, 7th Cavalry, will be Quartermaster.

(signed) G. A. Custer
Lieut. Col. 7th Cavalry

*

Fort Abr'm Lincoln, D. T.
June 13th, 1874

Samuel D. Hinman
  Springfield, Dakota.

The Santees should report to me at this place with as little delay as practicable. Telegraph me when they will start—the route taken and the number coming.

          (signed)   G. A. Custer
                    Brevet Maj. General, U. S. A.

*

St. Paul
6/13/1874

To General G. A. Custer
  Fort Lincoln.

One (1) ambulance ordered from Hancock.

                    Benj. C. Card
                    Chief Q. M.

*

Saint Paul, Minn.
6/13/74

To General Custer

Authority for advance payment to officers of your expedition granted by War Dept. What date shall paymaster arrive at Fort Lincoln?

                    O. H. Seward
                    Chief Paymaster Dept.

*

St. Paul, Minn.
6/13/1874

Commanding Officer
  Fort Lincoln

The medical business already attended to Drs. Williams, Allen and Bergen and a hospital steward will be sent to you. Lieut. Carland relieved and Varnum detailed in his stead. Lieut. Casey, Twenty-second

113

(22nd) Infantry can't go, his regiment is under orders to leave Dept. Dr. Davis' station is changed to Rice where he should go at once and relieve Allen to report to you.

O. D. Greene
A. A. G.

*

Fort Abr'm Lincoln, D. T.
June 15th, 1874

Assistant Adjutant General
    Department of Dakota
    Saint Paul.

A letter from Stanley contains the following.

I would not desire to be regarded as a timid counselor much less an alarmist but to give you a fair chance you ought to have four companies of Infantry X X X X if you choose to consider this you may give it as my official opinion that the Indians will fight. I send this not to ask for the additional infantry because I appreciate some of the embarrassments in the way of furnishing an increase of the present force. I also feel confident that I can hold my own against any force of hostile Indians, likely to be encountered. Were no obstacles in the way I would gladly have an addition to the infantry force, but do not wish to be understood as asking for more.

(signed)   G. A. Custer
            Brevet Major General, U. S. A.
            Commanding

*

Saint Paul, Minn.
6/15/74

Lieut. Col. Custer

There are two (2) odometers at Rice will you get them? Are the two (2) geologists at Lincoln? I have not seen them here.

Ludlow.

*

114

Saint Paul Minn.
6/15/74

Lieut. Col. G. A. Custer
7th Cavalry
Fort A. Lincoln, D. T.

The following telegram just received Chicago, June 14th, 1874. Every effort will be made to get forward the ordnance stores you mention. It is believed they will reach you in time. The Department Commander has telegraphed the Chief of Ordnance asking for the additional two hundred thousand (200,000) rounds ammunition to be sent here at once by rail; for this you must send in requisition in due form. It is really impossible to furnish you any more infantry for your expedition. The Twenty-second (22nd) is under orders to leave the Department; you are authorized to draw the company from Camp Hancock over to your post when you leave, directing it to leave a small guard behind to protect such public property as is left there. When your expedition returns, this company will be returned to Camp Hancock for winter quarters.

O. D. Greene[102]
A. A. General

*

Fort A. Lincoln, D. T.
June 16, 1874

Assistant Adjutant General
Department of Dakota
Saint Paul.

Captain Wheaton and company reported last night—Captain Sanger and company reported the previous day. Captain Wheaton's company

---

102.   St. Paul, Minn., 6/15/74

Bismarck
Lieut. Col. G. A. Custer
7th Cavalry, Ft. Lincoln

    The following telegram just received Chicago, June Fourteenth (14") Eighteen seventy-four (1874). Ordnance Department reports that ammunition for new carbines cannot be furnished. Hence this arm will not be furnished Lieut. Col. Custer's command.
       Signed R. C. Drum, A. A. G.   O. D. Greene
Gov't rate 56 words $1.68

R. C. Drum to G. A. Custer; original telegram in Lawrence A. Frost collection.

115

has but two officers the 1st Lieut. having been detailed at Pembina by Post Commander. The Rice companies will arrive here Saturday and with the Lincoln companies and infantry will encamp on Little Heart River; the expedition will move on the 25th.

(signed)   G. A. Custer
Brevet Major General, U. S. A.[103]

*

---

103. At this time many improbable stories about the mineral wealth in the Black Hills had been circulated along the frontier. There were references to mountains of solid gold within that strange country, and the story of a party of fourteen who had entered three years before, never to be seen again.

The *Bismarck Tribune* was elated over the government's proposed expedition, displaying even more than the enthusiasm they had expressed for the two expeditions organized by civilians; the Custer Expedition was receiving wide attention in the East mainly through *Tribune* reporting. Their reports of natives bringing in "hundreds of specimens of course [coarse] gold, some of them as large as walnuts" were emphasized by their comments in the June 14 issue:

"The American people need the country the Indians now occupy; many of our people are out of employment; the masses need some new excitement. The war is over, and the railroad building has been brought to a termination by the greed of the capitalists and the folly of the grangers; and the depression prevails on every hand. An Indian war would do no harm, for it must come sooner or later.

"Who does not recognize the necessity of our people? They must have something to do. Our cities are crowded with men out of employment, our factories are closed, our rolling mills idle—the industries of the country paralyzed. Custer's expedition may be the pebble which dropped in at an opportune moment will set the mighty sea of American thought in motion." (*Bismarck Tribune*, 14 June 1874.)

Sheridan had been receiving inquiries and comments as to the propriety of the military entering the Black Hills. Bishop William H. Hare, returning that summer from a trip to various Indian agencies, learned of Custer's proposed expedition. Hare protested to President Ulysses S. Grant in writing, but was ignored. Grant hadn't faced the fact that the Sioux were always on the warpath; further, he did not recognize that the public, suffering from a severe depression, was fed up with feeding what they considered to be a public nuisance: the Sioux. Grant found it politically expedient to permit the War Department to proceed with its plans.

The Indian raids in the early 1870s on the survey crew of the Northern Pacific Railroad had led Sheridan to conclude he could handle the Dakota Indians best if a military post could be established in the Black Hills.

Article 2 of the Treaty of 1868 states:

"The United States agrees . . . that no persons except those herein designated and authorized so to do, and except such officers, agents, and employes of the Government as may be authorized to enter upon Indian reservations in discharge of duties enjoined by law, shall ever be permitted to pass over, settle upon, or reside in the territory described in this article." Charles J. Kappler, *Indian Treaties* (New York, : Interland Printing Co., 1973, reprint of 1904 edition), pp. 998–1007.

In Article 1 of the treaty both the Indians and the government had pledged their honor to keep the peace: the government had promised to prevent any and all white intrusions on Indian land, and the Indians had pledged not to commit any depredations on the whites who were off Indian lands.

Springfield, D. T.
6/16/74

General Custer
Fort Lincoln

Twenty-five (25) Santee scouts are ready to start. Do you want their horses? Where shall they report? Gen. Stanley suggested that they go by rail from Yankton; answer and give full instructions.

S. A. Hinman

*

But the Indians had violated the treaty by their raids upon the Northern Pacific Railroad survey crews and upon white settlers. It appeared as if Sheridan's enterprise was in violation of the treaty. Historian Doane Robinson concluded that when it came to a decision, Sheridan had no recourse other than aiding the subjects of his government. Doane Robinson, *South Dakota Historical Collections* (Aberdeen, S.D.: South Dakota Historical Society), 2(1904):408.

Sheridan wanted to act within legal perimeters. Both Terry and Sherman had served on the commission that had drafted the terms of the Treaty of 1868, and both had a background in law. Quite wisely, Sheridan sent them a request for a clarification or interpretation of the document they had fathered. Though Sheridan's request was initiated on June 16, it was August 3 before it reached Sherman's desk. Terry's reply was as follows:

Headquarters Dept. of Dakota
Saint Paul, Minn., July 27, 1874

Respectfully returned to Headquarters Military Division of the Missouri.

I am unable to see that any just offense is given to the Indians by the expedition to the Black Hills. I cannot see that any of their rights, either those which they have possessed from the beginning or those which are secured to them by treaty, are invaded. From the earliest times the Government has exercised the right of sending exploring parties into the unceded Indian Territory—exploring parties of a military character, and this expedition is nothing more. It is a large party, it is true, but that it should be large is made necessary by the fact that certain bands of the Sioux are always ready to attack *small* parties either of civilians or troops. It was made large for the purpose of *preventing* hostilities.

The march of the expedition will be partly within and partly without the reservation established by the treaty of April 29, 1868; and it has been said that to send troops into or across that reservation is a violation of that treaty. To support this position reliance is placed upon the second article of the treaty, in which the United States "agrees that no person except those herein designated and authorized so to do, and except such officers, agents, and employes of the Government as may be authorized to enter upon the Indian reservations in discharge of duties enjoined by law, shall ever be permitted to pass over, settle upon, or reside in the territory described in this article, or in such territory as may be added to this reservation for the use of said Indians, and henceforth they will and do hereby relinquish all claims or right in and to any portion of the United States or Territories, except such as so embraced within the limits aforesaid, and except as hereinafter provided."

Fort Lincoln, D. T.
June 17, 1874

Assistant Adjutant General
  Department of Dakota
  Saint Paul, Minn.

The agent of the Santee Indians with whom Gen'l Stanley and myself had been communicating telegraphs me today that (25) twenty-five Santee Scouts are ready to go with the Expedition. From their knowledge of the country they would be extremely valuable with the expedi-

---

That this provision was intended to exclude from the reservation the military forces of the Government I cannot believe. As one of the Commissioners who made the treaty, I feel sure that the language of the section supports this construction. There are two classes excepted from the prohibition of residence, settlement and passage.

1st. Persons who are designated in and authorized by the treaty itself to reside, etc. 2nd. Such officers, agents and employes of the Government as may be authorized to enter upon the Indian reservations in discharge of duties enjoined by law. In subsequent sections the residence of an agent, a physician, a carpenter, blacksmith, farmer, engineer, miller, and schoolteacher—that is to say all the employes of the Government who are usually found on Indian reservations and who reside there for the benefit of the Indians—is specifically provided for. So that it is difficult to see what officers, agents, or employes are intended by the second exception unless it be the officers and men of the Army. So far as practice under the treaty can settle the construction to be given to it, the construction which I contend for has been settled, for since April 1869 three military posts have been established within the reservation—necessarily established for the protection of the Indian Agents and other employes of the Indian Bureau. And at the last session Congress appropriated thirty-thousand dollars for the building of two more such posts. The construction placed upon the treaty by the Bureau of Indian Affairs, I think, must be the same as mine for within a few days past it has asked for an escort of troops to accompany Bishop Hare into the heart of the reservation.

Again, by the eleventh article of the treaty the Indians stipulated "they will not in the future object to the construction of railroads, wagon roads, mail stations, or other works of utility or necessity which may be ordered or permitted by the laws of the United States. But should such roads or other works be constructed on the lands of their reservations the Government will pay the tribe whatever amount of damage may be assessed, etc."

It seems to me that the right to construct roads necessarily carries with it the right to make surveys, reconnaissances and explorations which are the prerequisites of their construction.

Aside from all this, can it be supposed that it was the intent of the treaty to set apart, in the heart of the national territory, a district nearly as great as the largest state east of the Mississippi River; two-thirds as large as the combined area of the six New England states, within which the Government should be forbidden to exercise the power, which it everywhere else possesses, of sending its military forces where they may be required?

The object of the expedition seems to be misunderstood both by Bishop Hare and by others. Bishop Hare in his telegram to the Secretary of the Interior says: "We are the marauders in this case." I trust that I shall not be considered as wanting in the respect which I know to be due to Bishop Hare, and which none would pay more cheerfully than I, when I say that I think that the term marauders is not happily chosen.

118

tion and I would like to have them, but they could only reach here in time by rail from Yankton, as suggested by General Stanley. The agent telegraphs if they shall start and by rail. If the Department Commander approves of their employment, please telegraph me, also to S. A. Hinman, agent of Santees at Springfield, Dakota to start them at once.

(signed)   G. A. Custer
Brevt. Maj. General, U. S. A.

*

Fargo, D. T.
6/17/74

General Custer
   Fort Lincoln

Will be at Fort Lincoln for advance payment this evening.

Rodney Smith
Paymaster

*

———————

A marauder is one who roves in quest of booty or plunder. Plunder is not the object of the expedition. Neither is it sent out for the purpose of ascertaining the mineral or agricultural resources of the Black Hills. It seeks neither gold, timber, non-arable land. It does seek routes of communication between the posts on the Missouri and those in the Department of the Platte which are west of the Black Hills and north of the Platte River. Should serious trouble arise, either with the hostile bands of Sioux or with the many semi-hostile Indians who spend a portion of the year on the reservation and trouble so serious that the combined action of the garrisons in the Department of the Platte and those on the Missouri would be necessary, is far from impossible—it will be very important that practicable routes through the Black Hills be known. It is the object of the expedition to find them.

With the exception of two geologists, a few—two or three, I think—correspondents of newspapers, and a photographer, no persons, except employes of the Government, have been permitted to accompany the troops. The geologists were permitted to go at the request of Professor Marsh of Yale College. It is understood that their special object is the Paleontology of the region in question.

Alfred H. Terry
Brigadier General
Commanding

On August 3, 1874, General W. T. Sherman attached the following endorsement:

Respectfully returned to the *Secretary of War*. I also was on the Commission to the Treaty of 1868 and agree with General Terry that it was not intended to exclude the United States from exploring the reservation for roads or for any other national purpose and I also agree with Gen. Terry that the language of the Treaty admits of such exploration.

W. T. Sherman
General

Letters received, Adjutant General's Office, Roll 152, National Archives, Washington, D.C.

119

Springfield, D. T.
6/18/74

General Custer
Fort Lincoln

Thirty-five (35) Santee scouts await your orders, answer.

(s'd)   Samuel A. Hinman

*

Fort Sully, D. T.
June 18, 1874

General Geo. A. Custer

John Brier is at Sioux City—You can reach him by telegraph care of
John Charles or Capt. C. W. Foster. Clement started to your post day
before yesterday. I will hunt George up if you want him. How many
did the Sioux lose in the fight?

D. S. Stanley
Col., 22nd Infantry.

*

St. Paul, Minn.
6/18/74

Lieut. Col. G. A. Custer
Fort A. Lincoln

How do you propose to mount the Santee scouts if they should come
by rail?

O. D. Greene
A. A. G.

*

Fort Lincoln, D. T.
June 18, 1874

Assistant Adjutant General
Department of Dakota

I can mount them on horses of men detailed with Gatling guns[104] and
as teamsters, also upon horses which can keep with column but are not

---

104. The Gatling gun was a hand-operated machine gun consisting of ten barrels into
which cartridges were fed by a hopper. One revolution of the crank fired ten shells. The

120

serviceable for either a charge or a long rapid march, horses which are unserviceable for hard cavalry service—I would like the scouts for their knowledge of the country, and their watchfulness in camp in detecting presence of hostile Indians near camp.

(signed)   G. A. Custer
Lieut. Colonel, 7th Cavalry

*

St. Paul
6/19/74

General G. A. Custer
Fort Lincoln

Rope will be sent by special messenger with carbines; no money for horse medicines.

Benj'n C. Card
Chief Qrmaster.

*

St. Paul
6/19/74

The Commanding Officer
Ft. Lincoln

We have ordered you the Santee scouts if they can be got here in time to forward to you and not delay you in starting. Card says the deficiency in mule harness will be fully made up by an invoice which should arrive at Bismarck tonight. Impossible to send you any more mules. There are two (2) horse boards buying for you. As fast as they get a car load they are sent here and forwarded at once. Sixteen (16) will reach Bismarck tonight and thirty-two (32) more on the twenty-fourth.

O. D. Greene
A. A. G.

*

---

gun was capable of firing 250 shots a minute with an effective range of 900 yards. Like a cannon, it was mounted on a two-wheeled carriage drawn by four horses. Heavy and unwieldy, it became quite apparent to Custer that Gatling guns were hardly the sort of armament to accompany fast-moving cavalry. Custer recalled these bad features and refused them before he traversed the rugged country leading to the valley of the Little Big Horn in 1876. *New York Times*, July 5, 1874.

Fort Lincoln, D. T.
June 19th, 1874

Colonel Ludlow.
  U. S. Army.
  St. Paul

The parties can be combined advantageously. G. B. Grinnell will take special charge of the fossil department. But one odometer at Fort Rice. Can't you procure another? Telegraph when you leave Saint Paul.

(signed)   G. A. Custer
Bv't Major General, U. S. A.

*

Saint Paul, Minn.
6/19/74

Lieut. Colonel Custer
  Fort Lincoln, D. T.

Professor Winchell with one assistant will go out as geologist for the expedition.[105] Will you arrange for him? Can Marsh's two (2) young men be directed by you to act in conjunction with him so as to consolidate the scientific party?[106]

Ludlow

*

Brainard, Minn.
6/20/74

General Custer
  Fort Lincoln

Forsythe, Grant, Wood, a correspondent and myself will be on your

---

105. Professor Newton H. Winchell, born December 17, 1839, in New York state, graduated from the University of Michigan in 1866. He was the state geologist of Minnesota.

106. Professor Othniel C. Marsh of Yale was invited by his friend Sheridan to accompany the expedition. The famous paleontologist was unable to go, but sent his young assistant, George Bird Grinnell, in his stead. Grinnell, in turn, asked Luther North to assist him. Charles Suchert and Clara LeVene, *O.C. Marsh, Pioneer in Paleontology* (New Haven, Conn.: Yale University Press, 1940), p. 142n; George B. Grinnell, *Two Great Scouts*, p. 339; and Marguerite Merington, *The Custer Story*, p. 211.

122

side of the river about 7 p.m. to-morrow Sunday.[107]

Ludlow

*

St. Paul, Minn.
6/20/74

Lieut. Col. G. A. Custer
    Fort Lincoln

Forsythe, Grant and Ludlow left to join you this morning. Ludlow has odometers.[108]

(signed)   O. D. Greene
A. A. G.

*

Saint Paul
6/20/74

General G. A. Custer
    Fort Lincoln

Will send horse medicines by special messenger.

Benj. C. Card
Chief Qrtm.

*

---

107. General George A. Forsyth was an aide-de-camp to Sheridan. Mr. W. H. Wood was the civilian assistant to Captain William Ludlow, chief engineer of the expedition. Colonel Frederick S. Grant was President Ulysses S. Grant's oldest son.

108. An odometer is an instrument used to measure distances when traveling; the leather-cased instrument was strapped to the wheel of the cart to measure revolutions. Sergeant Charles Becker rode the two-wheeled cart that carried one of the odometers; an ambulance carried the other. At the end of the day the two instruments were averaged and converted to miles. The readings were accepted as accurate if the terrain was level. If the terrain had been rough, the final figure was reduced from one to three percent. Donald Jackson, *Custer's Gold* (New Haven, Conn.: Yale University Press, 1966), p. 63.

123

Headqrs., Fort A. Lincoln, D. T.
June 20, 1874

Colonel Ludlow
    Department of Dakota

The odometer at Rice is unserviceable. You should bring two if practicable, also bring a supply of linen envelopes for dispatches.

(signed)   G. A. Custer
            Brevet Major General, U. S. A.

*

Fort Lincoln, D. T.
June 21st, 1874

Assistant Adjutant General
    Department of Dakota
    Saint Paul

Dr. Williams reports Dr. Bergen as wholly inexperienced in knowledge
of field duty. As the Hancock company is now on this side can I exchange Dr. Bergen with Dr. Porter? This change is recommended by
Dr. Williams.

(signed)   G. A. Custer
            Bv't. Maj. General, U. S. A.

*

Fort Sully, D. T.
6/22/74

General G. A. Custer
    Fort A. Lincoln

George leaves here today for Lincoln. He wants at least one hundred
and twenty-five dollars ($125) per month. He furnishes his own horses.

D. S. Stanley
Col., 22nd Infantry

*

St. Paul, Minn.
6/22/74

Lieut. Col. G. A. Custer
7th Cavalry
Fort Lincoln

Telegram yesterday from Rock Island Arsenal that the new carbines and ammunition were there with authority to issue; we at once asked for their immediate shipment here by rail expect them in time to ship Tuesday or Wednesday. The Department Commander instructs you to delay starting a day or two, if necessary in order to get them. He especially wants your command armed with the new carbines.

O. D. Greene
A. A. G.

*

Saint Paul, Minn.
6/22/74

Lieut. Col. G. A. Custer
7th Cavalry
Fort A. Lincoln

The Santee scouts will arrive here this p. m., and be forwarded tomorrow morning, reaching Bismarck Wednesday p. m. Have instructions and rations meet them there.

Forsythe's valise was shipped by Cook the omnibus man who said he had Forsythe's orders. The roll of bedding just came and will leave on tomorrow's train. The exchange of Dr. Bergen for Dr. Porter is not approved by Department Commander; will telegraph you when we know the time; the new carbines and ammunition will leave here on account of fatal illness in General Terry's family. Address all important messages to me.

O. D. Greene
A. A. G.

*

Saint Paul, Minn.
6/23/74

Lieut. Col. G. A. Custer
Fort A. Lincoln

Your Santee scouts twenty-eight (28) in number left here this morning. Telegram just received from Rock Island that the new carbines and ammunition will not arrive here till Thursday (25th); they will be forwarded hence same evening or next morning together with sixty four (64) horses. Wait their arrival.

O. D. Greene
A. A. G.

*

St. Paul, Minn.
6/26/74

Your new arms and ammunition have been delayed reaching here despite all we could do. They will leave this afternoon and reach Bismarck monday evening.

O. D. Greene
A. A. G.

*

St. Paul, Minn.
6/29/74

Lieut. Col. G. A. Custer
Fort Lincoln, D. T.

You are authorized to bring Private Hawley of C & Roth of K Company before the General Court of which Lieut. Varnum is J. A. for trial.

(signed)   O. D. Greene
A. A. G.

*

Fort Lincoln, D. T.
July 1st, 1874

Assistant Adjutant General
Saint Paul

As I had divided the ten companies of cavalry into two battalions and required the services of another field officer, I ordered Tilford up and he is now in command of five companies, Forsythe commanding the other five (5).

(signed)   G. A. Custer
Brevet Maj. General

*

126

Fort Abraham Lincoln, D. T.
July 1st, 1874

Assistant Adjutant General
  Department of Dakota
  Saint Paul

The Black Hills Expedition will move tomorrow morning. The new arms give great satisfaction. The Expedition considering its number is the most thoroughly equipped, armed and best organized force I have seen on the plains.

        (signed)   G. A. Custer
                     Brevet Maj. General

*

Fort A. Lincoln, D. T.
July 1st, 1874

General O. D. Greene
  Saint Paul

We get off tomorrow in tiptop condition. Any dispatches arriving tomorrow can overtake us, as we only camp twelve miles from here.

        (s'd)   G. A. Custer
                   Brevet Maj. General

*

Conclusions

The military reconnaissance of the Black Hills was a complete success. A route was established from Fort Abraham Lincoln in the Dakota Territory to Bear Butte in the Black Hills, and the area surrounding Bear Butte was explored, mapped, and scientifically investigated. A photographic record was made of the expedition, and gold was discovered.

The newspaper correspondents accompanying the expedition, whose interests always tended toward the sensational, played up the gold discovery at a time the country was recovering from the Panic of 1873. With unemployment and poverty at a new high, the politicans and the people welcomed the diversion.

Gold discovery was heralded, but few recognized the immense value of the scientific information that was obtained. Few appreciated the skill required to organize and guide a large force into a hitherto unexplored segment of the country that had never been successfully penetrated because there had been no known entrance. It had been rumored that a force of 5,000 Indian warriors would repulse any attempt to approach the Black Hills.

Custer's reconnaissance-in-force of over 1,000 men was expected to handle any situation confronting it. Because Custer professed his pacific intentions by visiting Sioux delegations prior to leaving Fort Lincoln and by displaying his purpose while on the march and when in contact with Sioux within the hills, he was able to complete his mission without Indian confrontation.

Not enough credit has been given to Custer for his respect for the Indians and for his knowledge of the Indian temperament. That his assignment was successfully completed without bloodshed cannot be attributed to luck. He had established a rapport with the Indians: he was open with the Indians and they with him.

On July 26, Custer gave a demonstration of his pacific intentions toward the Indians when he captured a small village of Sioux his scouts had discovered within the Black Hills. Forsyth's report of the action as forwarded to Sheridan and published in the *Chicago Daily Tribune*, August 26, 1874, read: "Taking the scouts and about 50 men with him, Gen. Custer moved quietly down upon them, and giving strict orders they should not be harmed unless they showed fight, sent forward a white flag by one of the interpreters, and followed it almost instantly."

When a reporter from the *Bismarck Tribune* interviewed Custer on September 1, he asked: "I presume you were disappointed in not having a brush with the Sioux?"

Custer replied, "Yes, I was somewhat disappointed for, though I had sent pacific messages and had taken every precaution to avoid hostilities, I had reason to anticipate trouble. I was disappointed, and am heartily glad of it. Some thought I courted an engagement—such was not the case, and I congratulate myself and the country on the return of the expedition without bloodshed."[109]

Earlier, on May 19, he had written to actor Lawrence Barrett that "the expedition is entirely peaceful in its object it being the intention to explore the country known as the Black Hills and gain some knowledge as to the nature of the latter.... I say that our object is a peaceful one but I have no idea that our trip will be so.... The Indians have long opposed all efforts of white men to enter the Black Hills and I feel confident that the Sioux will combine their entire strength and endeavor to oppose

---

109. *Bismarck Tribune*, September 1, 1874.

us. I will have a well-equipped force, however, strong enough to [take] care of itself . . . ." (George A. Custer to Lawrence Barrett, Library of Congress.)

The *St. Paul Pioneer* echoed these sentiments by printing: "The purposes of this expedition are not military or aggressive. They are peaceable and exclusively in the interest of science. . . . Of the peaceable intentions of the government all the tribes have been notified, and they have been assured that they will not be molested or disturbed in the least degree, provided they do not commence hostilities."[110]

Prior to entry into the Black Hills Custer had been visited many times by various Sioux chiefs. The more eloquent leaders would tell him how dishonest Indian agents cheated their people out of food the government owed them. Libbie Custer recalled how Indians would ask her husband to keep the white men out of the Black Hills in order to prevent war. They said they would fight for the land that was theirs. After they had gone, Custer turned to Libbie and said: "The Government must keep its promises to the Indians."[111] Libbie went on to say that Custer "was a sincere friend of the reservation Indian."[112] He was tolerant of them and their way of living: he studied their habits, sign language, religious beliefs, and mode of warfare, and applied such to his advantage. He respected them as highly skilled adversaries. The knowledge and information he acquired led him to conclude, "If I were an Indian, I often think I would greatly prefer to cast my lot among those of my people adhered to the free open plains rather than submit to the confined limits of a reservation, there to be recipient of the blessed benefits of civilization, with its vices thrown in without stint or measure."[113]

Custer had been quite concerned about the excursions of white men into the Black Hills. In March 1874 an ad appeared in the *Bismarck Tribune* asking for supplies and ammunition to aid a party of fifty men who wanted to enter the Black Hills in mid-April for the purpose of prospecting. Custer advised Terry

---

110. George A. Custer to Lawrence Barrett, May 1, 1874 (see footnote 97 for a full text of this letter); and *St. Paul Pioneer*, June 26, 1874.

111. Elizabeth B. Custer, "General Custer and the Indian Chiefs," p. 408.

112. Elizabeth B. Custer, *Boots and Saddles*, p. 226.

113. George A. Custer, *My Life on the Plains* (New York: Sheldon and Co. 1874), p. 18.

of his concern; Terry responded by ordering Custer to prevent such irresponsible acts and to use force, if necessary. Once it was known that Custer meant business, plans for the proposed expedition were prudently abandoned.

Following the Custer expedition into the Black Hills, hordes of white men entered the area illegally. Custer's troopers arrested many of them, turning the miscreants over to civilian authorities for prosecution. The civil courts in that area were sympathetic to the civilians arrested and, just as quickly, released them.

Did Custer violate the Treaty of 1868? Sherman didn't think so, and he helped shape the treaty, as did Terry. (Terry had even a more important part in drafting the treaty.) Both concluded the expedition was necessary and legal. Both ordered Custer to plan and lead the undertaking.

Whether Custer took the two practical miners along on his own or at the suggestion of Sheridan or Terry is unknown. Though the discovery of gold was emphasized by the newspaper correspondents accompanying the expedition, Custer played it down. Having been raised on a farm, he displayed his greatest interest in the agricultural advantages the area offered. Its potential for farming and grazing, not for mining, was emphasized by him. That he did not take advantage of the gold discovery is evident when reviewing the list of claims staked out at the site: Custer's name is not on that list.

In a final interview Custer stated: "Too much cannot be said in favor of the agricultural worth of the valleys in the Black Hills. No country in the world is superior for stock growing—the grazing is unsurpassed, the valleys are sheltered from driving storms, the snow fall is evidently light, the rain fall abundant."[114]

The *St. Paul Pioneer*, in a summation published in its issue of September 20, 1874, concurred with Custer's remark about the agricultural potential of the Black Hills. The *Pioneer* warned that as far as precious metals went "the country was neither an Eldorado or barren," then gave its readers some final advice: "Don't go to the Black Hills before they are opened to settlement by the United States; then, if gold-mining 'does not pay' you will find a pleasant and happy home among the thriving

---

114. *Bismarck Tribune*, September 2, 1874.

and varied industry of the busy settlers all around you, safe under protection of U.S. military posts."

Index

mapping, photography, and scientific studies of, xxii–xxiii, 129; Custer's desire to explore, 9–10, 11; public attitude toward, 10; Indians' attitude toward, 10; suitability of, for sheep raising, 41; suitability of, for agriculture, 58, 67, 132; Calhoun's feelings on leaving, 75; route of expedition through, 78–79; Custer's comments on natural resources in, 79–80

Black Hills Expedition, Custer's calculations on economics of, xvii–xviii, 92–93; logistics and supply of, xvii, xviii, xxi, 4, 14, 15, 17, 20, 21, 24, 29, 88, 91–95, 98–100, 102–103, 105, 107, 109–115, 124; Custer ordered to organize,xviii; description of expeditionary force, xx–xxi; purposes of, xx, 103–104, 119, 130–32; accomplishments of, xxii–xxiii, 129; sightings of and contacts with Indians during, xxiii, 33, 35, 37, 54, 55, 64–66, 73, 80; gold rush following, contributed to Little Big Horn tragedy, xxiii–xxiv; appointments on staff of commanding officer, 8–9; citizens accompanying, 9; Calhoun's observations on, 9–12; roster of officers, 12–13; order of march in, 15–19; plan of camp in, 47; security on the March of, 18, 19; meals eaten, 20n; Indian scouts with, 23, 106n; official reports on, by Custer, 34–35, 62–69, 77–80; daily distances traveled during, 34, 36n, 48; deaths occurring during, 42, 49–51, 74, 85; salaries of civilian employees, 52n; enjoyed by soldiers, 56; discovery of gold during, 56, 59, 60, 68, 72, 79–80, 86n, 120, 132; Custer congratulated on, 87n; Custer's expectations of, 96–98; political factors behind, 116n; Custer comments on preparedness of, 127. *See also* Treaty of 1868

Bloody Knife, 25, 38n, 54, 64–65, 71, 80, 106
Box Elder Creek, 84
Bozeman Expedition, 11, 66
Bozeman Trail, xvi
Brier, John, 120
Brown, Hiram E., 21
Bull Bear (Bull Neck), 33n
Bunting, Clark W., 75n
Bureau of Indian Affairs, 118

Calhoun, Charlotte (Lottie), xxiv, xxviii
Calhoun, Frederick, xxiv, 77n
Calhoun, James, preservation of expedition diary of, xxiv; childhood and education, xxiv–xxv; military training and career, xxv; tried for "rascality," xxvi–xxviii; testimonials regarding character of, xxxvi–xxvii; marriage of, xxviii; travels of, xxviii; views on Black Hills, xxix; death and burial of, xxix–xxx; feelings on leaving for expedition, 2, 6–7; views on military personnel, 2–5; on soldiers around the campfire, 8; observations on Black Hills Expedition, 9–12; on preparedness of expedition, 22; comments on advancement of civilization, 40; feelings on leaving Black Hills, 75; 46
Campbell, Sarah ("Aunt Sally"), 66n
Camp Grant, xxvi, xxvii
Camp Hancock, 5, 112, 115
Camp Thomas, xxvii
Camp Warner, xxv
Cannonball River, 26, 27, 104, 105
Capitol Butte, 38
Card, Benjamin C., 102, 110, 112, 121, 123
Carland, John, 113
Carlin, William P., 105
Carrington, H. B., xv
Casey, L. F., 111, 113
Castle Creek, 56, 60, 66
Castle Valley, 43, 53n, 56
Cavee Yard, 82n, 83n
Chance, Josiah, 5, 12, 15, 57, 84, 101

136

137

138

on, 2–5; public attitude toward, 2–3; contributions to Westward movement, 4–5; American, compared with European, 7–8
Missouri River, xix, 20n, 93, 100, 119n
Molloy, Dan, 85
Mount Pleasant Military Academy, xxv
Moylan, Myles, 12

Newel, Dan, 62n
Noonan, John, 71
North, Luther, 122n
Northern Cheyenne Indians, xviii
Northern Pacific Railroad, xxviii, 88, 108n, 116n, 117n
Nowlan, Henry J., 88

Odometer, 114, 123, 124
O'Gara, Edward, 73
Okandanda Indians, xiv
One Stab, 55, 59, 59–66, 70
Owl Butte, 81

Panic of 1873, 129
Park, Mungo, 25
Parker, Watson, 70
Platte River, xvi, xix
Poland, J. D., 87n
Porter, Joseph Y., 111, 124, 125
Powder River, 37, 38, 66, 82
Powers, Fred W., 9, 36n
Progulske, Ronald R., xxii
Prospect Valley, 32, 33n, 34, 36n, 62, 82

"Rascal Pat," 5
Red Cloud, xv, xvi, 54, 66
Red Cloud Agency, xix
Reed, Emma, 24n, 77n
Ree Indians. *See* Arikara Indians
Reynolds, Charlie, xxi, 37, 39, 61, 62n, 67, 69, 86n
Roach, George H., 13
Roberts, Harry, 83n
Rock Island Arsenal, 88, 89, 109, 125
Roller, William, 49
Ross, Horatio Nelson, xxii, 32n, 52n, 56n, 60n, 61n, 72n

Roth, Theodore, 126
Running Antelope, xix

Sanger, Louis H., xxi, 1, 13, 15, 116
Santee Indians, 23n, 107, 112, 113, 117, 119, 120, 121, 125
Seward, O. H., 113
Sheridan, Philip H., xvii, xix, xxi, xxiii, 10, 61n, 86n, 95, 96, 104, 110
Sherman, William T., xvi, xvii, 117n, 119n
Short Pine Hills, 80n
Shoshone Indians, 23n
Shyenne River. *See* Cheyenne River
Sioux Indians, xiii, xiv, xv, xvi, xviii, xix, xxiii, xxix, 23n, 55, 65, 80n, 87n, 100, 103, 104, 106, 116n, 119n, 130; Brule Sioux, siv; Ogallala Sioux, 54; Teton-Dakota Sioux, xiv, xvii
Sitting Bull, xvi, 80n
Skunk's Head, 33n
Slave Butte, 80, 81
Slim Butte, 31, 102
Smith, Algernon E., xxx, 8, 12, 17, 21, 83n
Smith, Edward P., 72n
Smith, Edward M., 87n
Smith, John M., xviii, xix
Smith, John W., 61n
Smith, Rodney, 119
Snow, Antelope Fred, 31n, 37n, 56, 62n
South Butte, 82
Spotted Tail, xvi, 66
Spotted Tail Agency, xix, 69
Springfield carbines, 10, 13, 19, 89, 103, 109, 115, 121, 125, 126
Springfield muskets, 14, 103
Standing Rock Agency, xix, 96, 100
Stanley, David S., xxviii, 84, 105, 111, 112, 117, 118, 119, 124
Stempker, Charles, 83, 85, 86
Stoneman, George, xxvi
Stout, Edward, 25, 27
Sturgis, Samuel, xvii, 87n

Terry, Alfred, xvii, xx, 10, 87n, 88, 96, 98, 101, 104, 108n, 109, 117n, 119n, 125, 132

139